GREAT LEADERS ALWAYS FOLLOW

THE PARADOX OF GREAT LEADERSHIP

Rob Fontenot

WESTBOW
PRESS®
A DIVISION OF THOMAS NELSON
& ZONDERVAN

Copyright © 2018 Rob Fontenot.

All rights reserved. No part of this book may be used or reproduced by any means, graphic, electronic, or mechanical, including photocopying, recording, taping or by any information storage retrieval system without the written permission of the author except in the case of brief quotations embodied in critical articles and reviews.

This book is a work of non-fiction. Unless otherwise noted, the author and the publisher make no explicit guarantees as to the accuracy of the information contained in this book and in some cases, names of people and places have been altered to protect their privacy.

Scripture taken from the King James Version of the Bible.

WestBow Press books may be ordered through booksellers or by contacting:

WestBow Press
A Division of Thomas Nelson & Zondervan
1663 Liberty Drive
Bloomington, IN 47403
www.westbowpress.com
1 (866) 928-1240

Because of the dynamic nature of the Internet, any web addresses or links contained in this book may have changed since publication and may no longer be valid. The views expressed in this work are solely those of the author and do not necessarily reflect the views of the publisher, and the publisher hereby disclaims any responsibility for them.

Any people depicted in stock imagery provided by Thinkstock are models, and such images are being used for illustrative purposes only. Certain stock imagery © Thinkstock.

ISBN: 978-1-9736-1791-4 (sc)
ISBN: 978-1-9736-1792-1 (hc)
ISBN: 978-1-9736-1793-8 (e)

Library of Congress Control Number: 2018901403

Print information available on the last page.

WestBow Press rev. date: 2/7/2018

ACKNOWLEDGEMENTS

I want to give a special thank you to my wife and children. Without their love and sacrifice, this book would not exist. Because of them, I have a more profound drive and desire to become a great leader.

I also want to say thank you to many others who played essential roles in the creation of this book:

- Tammy McCray who introduced me to many of the leaders I had the privilege to interview
- Brenda Anderson who unknowingly re-inspired my love for writing
- Carly Dotson and Rebecca Rice who helped in the early stages of editing and content feedback
- Susan Yauck who provided great editorial advice at mid-stage
- Kim Logan who introduced me to Buba Turner
- All of the leaders who graciously allowed me to interview them and allowed me to use their wisdom and leadership insights

PREFACE

Throughout the process of writing this book, I have had many people ask me why I was writing it and why I felt qualified to write a book on leadership. I will start things out by addressing both of those excellent questions.

The reason for writing this book is twofold. I am a student of leadership, and I know that there is no better way to learn than to teach. The second reason started with a challenge. I was never fond of reading, and few books captivated me while growing up. After graduating college, I did not immediately get into reading books on business, leadership, or any other topic for that matter.

It wasn't until I saw a post on social media that the world's top business leaders read at least 12 books a year. Knowing what I wanted out of my career, I already saw myself at a disadvantage since reading was not a practice of mine. To change that, I challenged myself to "catch up" by reading 30 business or leadership books from August 2016 to August 2017. I fell in love with reading, and by May 2017 I had read 35 books on business or leadership.

What I learned from some of the world's greatest business leaders, thought leaders, and professors cut my learning curve, and I was able to apply much of what I learned into my profession. Leading a global team, I found these new insights to be incredibly beneficial as a leader. I was able to learn from other's mistakes, insights, and experiences and avoid wasted years of doing things the wrong way until I figured it out myself. I am far from perfect (as my team will likely tell you), but I know that I am much further along than I would have been otherwise.

In the midst of the incredibly positive year of reading, something was missing. Much of the material I read had pointed to something insightful. Then it hit me. I was inspired to write this book to share the insight I had. So what happened? What was the insight?

I noticed a gap in mainstream teachings on leadership. Many of the materials out there are on the characteristics and competencies of leaders. While this is necessary and beneficial, it is not complete. There is also material on the difference between managers and leaders. Again, another helpful delineation, but it still does not fill the gap. In all of this material, it is clear what a leader looks like and what makes individuals want to follow a leader. What is less clear, and what I believe to be a paradox of great leadership, is what determines how great an individual is at *leading* by how well they *follow*.

Do not get me wrong, the concepts in this book are not all new. The reason why I felt compelled to write this is I have yet to find a comprehensive overview of what great leaders follow and *how* they do it. It is my firm belief that great leaders follow all seven of the topics I cover, and it is when they stop following them or stop following them in the right way that great leaders falter.

To address the second question of why I felt qualified to write this book, I don't. At the time of writing this, I am still a relatively young leader. I know that my limited experience is not sufficient to write a book. However, each point I make in this book comes from either experience, observations of great leaders, or shared insights from great leaders. Knowing that my personal experience would be insufficient, I sought out exceptional leaders from across the globe and interviewed them on the subject of leadership. Each leader I spoke with addressed many or all of the aspects which I will cover in the next eight chapters. Each of them provides compelling stories from their own experience which complement the points I make throughout each section.

I know that we are all busy individuals, so I was intentional about keeping the material short, sweet, and to the point. I do not like to read books that say the same thing, multiple ways, and I will respect your time by not doing the same. I have personally learned so much and have grown significantly through the process of writing this book and learning from many exceptional leaders from across the world. I hope that you too will benefit from the points of the ensuing chapters and the lessons and stories of the great leaders I had the privilege to learn from.

INTRODUCTION

The Hebrew language is a language of symbolism. Each letter and number in Hebrew has a meaning. In Hebrew, the number 7 represents completion. "For in six days, the Lord made heaven and earth, the sea, and all that in them is, and rested the seventh day."[1] Our seven-day week is based on this event. In the spirit of the Hebrew meaning for the number 7, I aim to provide a *complete* view of why and what great leaders follow in the first seven chapters.

The number 8 in Hebrew represents new beginnings. With all of the corruption and negative press around CEOs over the years, the scandals in big corporations, and the withering trust of corporate leaders in America, leadership is in desperate need of a new beginning. We need a generation of leaders who can remove the stain their forbearers left behind. In chapter eight I will conclude by showing you *how* great leaders follow. Even if you have the first seven principles down, if the eighth is missing, you will inevitably not be remembered as a great leader.

The experiences of our lives shape who we are and our views of the world. When you see leaders acting in a certain way, the belief you form is that those actions are how leaders are supposed to behave. The thoughts, words, and actions of leaders subconsciously tell us that we should also think, speak, and act in those same ways for us to obtain some measure of success. The experiences that you create for your followers will always be impactful, but whether that impact is negative or positive is up to you.

As a leader, it is your job to provide direction for those you are trying to lead. The old expression goes, "if the blind lead the blind, both shall fall into the ditch."[2] And a leader who does not *have* direction cannot *provide* direction. To be a great leader, you must have a vision worth following, and that vision needs to focus on something greater than yourself. The type of vision that people rally around is never about the amount of money they can make. It is about the impact they get to make.

David Ng, CEO of GoGame in Singapore, says that an organization's vision and value proposition must go hand in hand. If your vision is not to add value to your customers, it is not a good vision. As human beings, we need purpose in life. We crave it. No amount of material wealth that can satisfy this craving, and there are far too many examples of depressed rich people to validate this truth. It is purpose that gives life meaning. Even if the money never comes pouring in, a life of purpose will lead to you a fulfilled life. In business, it is purpose that creates loyalty and buy-in. It is purpose that allows people to not only see you as their boss but *call you their leader*. It is *what you follow* that will make others want to follow you, and it is *how* you follow that will determine your leadership legacy.

Great leaders know the importance of observation,

open-mindedness, and humility. Turning a blind eye to corporate ethics or failure to follow organizational values will quickly erode a culture that you have worked hard to build. Not keeping an eye on your industry, and the changes in it will lead to missed opportunities and unnoticed threats. Close-mindedness will close off the likelihood of innovation in your organization and cascade a culture void of innovation deep into your organization. This sort of attitude will eventually choke off your communication flow because your organization will quickly realize that their feedback will not be heard, received, or welcomed.

Additionally, it takes a humble leader to allow the leaders they are developing within the organization to lead up. The CEO cannot see everything, and there is a real reliance on those within the organization who can provide insightful feedback. Without the humility to accept input that might contradict the current course of action, it is likely that the organization will remain rowing in the wrong direction, and possibly right off the edge of the cliff.

Leaders make decisions, and they follow through on those decisions. As mentioned before, leaders do keep an open mind to pivoting or changing course, but great leaders do not hesitate to make decisions. In an interview, Brian Krzanich, CEO, shared some of his successes and failures in decision making. When he took the role, Krzanich knew that there was more to the Compute industry than the traditional PC business. There were direct investments made in the mobile market due to the revenues the likes of Apple were making on their Smartphone and iPad sales. Intel knew that they were late to the mobile market but hoped to catch up by buying their way into the tablet market.

On the other hand, Intel felt that they were well positioned to be an early leader in the Data Center and Internet of Things industries. Although some of the client computing investments, like tablets and 3D cameras, failed, the ventures in the data center and the IoT were very profitable. Intel pulled out of tablets, re-positioned their 3D camera investments, and continue to grow their new business units. How has Krzanich been able to grow Intel from a single-focused, 45 billion dollar company to a diversified "data company" with revenues now up to $60 billion? Making bold decisions. In his own words, "No CEO ever says that they wish they took longer to make a decision. Executives need to be comfortable with diving headfirst into a problem instead of delaying their decision-making process. I believe that, now more than ever, we all sit and ponder and worry and debate our decisions for far too long. What we really need to do is get the company moving in a direction and be willing to constantly review and be willing to modify our decisions."[3]

Another critical aspect of leadership is communication. Great leaders know that communicating vision or direction once will not suffice if they seek to see the organization be successful in the long run. Staying with the example of Intel, there have been some changes since Krzanich took over the CEO role. Intel invested in mobile and new client computing technology and then got out of it. Intel invested in two major business units and hired executives away from competitors. There were roughly 11,000 jobs lost in the reorganization of Intel in 2016, and investments were shifting around frequently. In the course of all this internal disruption, how did Intel get anything accomplished, let alone grow revenues year over year as it did? The answer is communication. Krzanich and his staff did a great job of letting employees know what the changes in direction meant for the entire business. He showed how the new investments complemented the traditional business and vice versa. He showed how all aspects of Intel's business created synergy into what Intel calls the "virtuous cycle of growth."

In turbulent seas, the calming of the storm is found through frequent, consistent communication. And even in the calm nature of smooth waters, it is that same consistent communication that allows the organization to stay on point and make the necessary adjustments with the slightest changes in the wind.

Lastly, every great leader strives to win; however, every great leader also knows that to win is meaningless if they do not follow the rules. What happens to a great baseball player like Barry Bonds when the world found out that he was breaking the rules by taking performance-enhancing drugs? His reputation is tarnished, he loses followers, and all of his prior accomplishments are brought into question. The value they once had is now greatly diminished, if intact at all. Whether in sports, business, or life, it is not always about *what* you do, but it *is* always about *how* and *why* you do it. As the old saying goes, "For what is a man profited, if he shall gain the whole world, and lose his own soul?"[4]

CHAPTER 1
GREAT LEADERS FOLLOW ANOTHER GREAT LEADER

When great leaders are asked about the many influences on their lives, I'm sure there will be multiple examples of people or events that inspired the individuals to do something great. However, when you drill down, there is usually one or a few prominent figures who stand above the others in shaping the emerging, great leader. These great influences are always other great leaders.

Mark Zuckerberg

When Mark Zuckerberg was interviewed by Michael Arrington at TechCrunch Disrupt back in 2013, he told of how Bill Gates was his hero growing up. The reason, he states, is that "Bill Gates ran one of the most mission-driven companies I can think of. Microsoft had a great mission, to put a computer on every desktop and in every home." It was Bill Gates and his focus on his vision to enable others that inspired Mark Zuckerberg. The motivation of Bill Gates wasn't money. His mission statement wasn't "become a billionaire by taking over a large section of the tech industry."[1] No, he was motivated by something more significant than himself that drove him ultimately to succeed.

It was this selfless ambition and desire to give away power to others that inspired Facebook's founder and CEO to follow his hero in achieving something great for others as well. As of the day this was written, Facebook's mission is "Give people the power to build community and bring the world closer together."[2] Facebook's mission statement is not about how much money Mark Zuckerberg and his company can make; it's about people and community. His actions prove that his motivation is not self-gain. In another act of following his hero, Mark also joined Bill Gates' Giving Pledge. This is a commitment by the world's wealthiest people to give most of their wealth to philanthropy.

Buba Turner

Buba Turner is the director of IT Enterprise Management and Strategy at Boeing. She grew up with a father who was in leadership positions since she was born. Her late father was a presidential adviser in the Zambian government, and you could say that leadership was in her blood. Her leadership journey started in her elementary school in Zambia, Africa, where each class had a "class captain" of sorts, which they called a "prefect." Buba held this role through elementary school and high school. She was even the captain of her high school debate team.

Buba describes her leadership journey as a natural progression. She had early signs of being a leader and viewed as a leader by her peers and teachers from a very young age. Although what some would call a natural-born-leader, Buba credits much of her success and growth to great leaders who brought her along with them and helped her develop and grow. Bringing others up with her is a leadership behavior she emulates today due to the fantastic mentors she had along the way.

Buba's mentors saw leadership potential in her and put her on a path of upward growth in the organization. Several of her mentors brought her with them to executive level meetings so she could observe, listen, and grow. Watching and listening are how Buba learns best and having the opportunity to watch and listen to the articulations and collaborations of her senior managers proved to be incredibly insightful. Even the ability to practice reading body language provided insights into how leaders responded to the varying dynamics of the conversation.

Buba was very intentional about having a variety of mentors. She is often asked why she did not choose only one mentor and if she ever became confused by the different and possibly contradicting advice and information. Buba is a leader, and great leaders do not shy away from making decisions. When it came to receiving diverse input from mentors, it allowed Buba to decide. She was able to take it all in and determine what was relevant to her, what resonated, and what advice she considered beneficial or applicable.

Buba's actions in seeking advice and input from multiple sources is consistent with great leaders. Great leaders know they can learn something from everyone, even if you learn what not to do. Choosing only one mentor, even if a great one, will limit your perspectives, growth, and effectiveness as a leader. Great leaders surround themselves with other great leaders because they know that "iron sharpens iron."[3] In a similar way, great leaders also develop and grow other great leaders. Just as Buba's mentors gave her opportunities to go with them for her growth, Buba now does the same for those she mentors in her organization.

Buba told me a great story of when the principles of this lesson really clicked for her. "My CIO invited me to go over my program and wanted to see how my areas were doing, and I would go to present alone." He asked her, "Buba, did you put that entire presentation together by yourself?"

"No," she replied.

"How many people participated in helping pull this presentation together for you?" "Well, I had this person from that area and that person from this other area who helped," she responded.

Then the CIO asked, "Well, they obviously know their area well enough to pull all of this together, right?"

"Well, yeah."

Finally, he asked, "Well, why aren't you bringing them along to present their area?"

That's when the lightbulb went off. She instantly thought about her mentors and how they brought her along, yet she was not doing the same for her employees.

What Buba took away from that experience is that she had the opportunity to empower her team to present their areas for themselves and to let them get the credit for it. They deserved it, and they were the ones executing the work every day. By following the actions of her mentors and the advice of her CIO, she learned what all great leaders need to know. Great leaders develop other great leaders, and the lesson here is that bringing your people along with you allows you another avenue for grooming your future leaders.

Jesus of Nazareth

Jesus was the ultimate servant leader. He studied in the Jewish temple and engaged with the religious scholars and leaders from a very early age. Although being so well-educated, as an adult, Jesus surrounded Himself with very common followers. His closest, most dedicated followers were fishermen, a tax collector, and men of other ordinary occupations. He, unlike many hiring managers today, saw past their résumés and looked at their characters as the essential qualification for being His future successors, to carry on His vision, and execute His mission. Like many inspired leaders of today, Jesus knew what leadership was supposed to look like, and He set out to change the corrupt ways of that time. Does the struggle to rid corruption from powerful entities sound familiar? With Enron, WorldCom, and a host of other examples, it's no wonder that Blanchard's very first sentence in his book *Lead like Jesus* is that the world is most certainly in need of a different leadership role model.[4]

What did Jesus do that applies to today's leaders? In leadership there are two important, broad topics to consider for leaders to become successful or great. Most leaders are consumed with topic number one: the here and now. With pressures from Wall Street, shareholders, and other external forces, you can somewhat sympathize with the lack of quality decisions leaders make at times. Bad choices for the wrong reasons are never excusable, but you can understand how these pressures can play a role.

Jesus had many temptations as a leader. He was promised all the wealth, perks, and benefits a person could think of if He would only submitted to another's vision. This would have circumvented the mission Jesus was working to carry out. Even with all this life had to offer, Jesus didn't cave. Even when death loomed, Jesus held resolute to His mission. He would not give in to the desires of corrupted individuals.

The second broad topic is the *there and later*. The focus of this issue is vision and succession. Jesus had a vision for how things were supposed to operate around Jerusalem, and He was not shy about letting leaders know where they fell short. His criticisms were mostly due to the arrogance of those leaders. It was to such an extent that they could not be taught. Nor would they take advice that went against their current way of thinking. They allowed their supposed knowledge and arrogance to drive them to foolishness and close-mindedness. Can you think of similar stories about modern-day leaders?

Jesus also developed and equipped eleven of the greatest leaders and successors the world might ever know. It's all too often today that when the charismatic leader leaves the company, things start to fall apart. Howard Schultz leaving Starbucks and Steve Jobs leaving Apple are two prominent examples in recent history. Did this happen after Jesus died? No. In fact, the small organization of followers that Jesus had when He died substantially grew as His eleven successors built one of the largest organizations in the world.

How did Jesus accomplish what so many of today's business leaders fail to do? He left His successors with a sustainable vision. He equipped His successors and showed them how to develop successors of their own. He gave His successors a mission that was selfless and focused on helping others. And the vision, plans, and guidance were all well-documented for continuity. There is no arguing these principles, and their relevance for today, for leaders who want their organizations to succeed long-term.

What Jesus was able to accomplish in showing the people of Israel and the surrounding nations in how leaders were supposed to treat people is something all leaders today should note. Jesus did not have "executive elevators" (even though there were no elevators two thousand years ago) that allowed Him to avoid so-called commoners. He did not stay hidden away in His office, making Himself inaccessible to those who needed Him. No, He was a personal leader. He stood before masses of people and poured Himself into others with a genuine care and love for people that is matchless. He didn't see classes of people; He only saw *people*. Jesus knew what many who gain leadership titles forget: we're all just people. We all bleed, and one day we all die.

Why did He attract such a following in that day, and why does Jesus still have millions of followers today? It's simple. Jesus gave his life to a single mission and purpose. He relentlessly followed a vision and regardless of what others said or did to Him, He followed through on His purpose.

He taught people how to live personally and professionally in ways that set his followers up for ultimate success. He taught people that true leadership started and ended with their heart. He taught people how to lead their own lives and be leaders of others.

How do we know that following the example and leadership of Jesus is still applicable for today? Let us look at an example of a great leader who still follows the teachings of Jesus and stands as proof of its effectiveness and timelessness.

Scott Sessions

Scott Sessions is the Senior Vice President of Mountain Alarm, a Utah-based, fire and security company. Scott proves that you don't need to have your name in lights or in the history books to be a great leader. He is full of leadership wisdom and shared with me many insights into what has made him and his organization successful.

We'll talk later about the culture that Scott and the leadership team has developed and maintained at Mountain

Alarm, but one firm stance that he and Mountain Alarm takes is that the people come first. Love is a big part of the culture at Mountain Alarm, and that principle of putting others first, in love, comes from the teaching of Jesus. In the book of 1st John, there's a statement made that followers of Jesus love Him because He first loved us. As leaders, we don't automatically get the respect and love of our people because of our title. To get it, we must first show it.

When Lou Holtz was offered the head football coaching position at Notre Dame, the Athletic Director told him that he was going to introduce Lou as their coach but not as their leader. What he said to Lou was that the *team* would decide if Lou was their leader; he would have to earn it. That's exactly right. Titles don't grant you respect and love. Leaders must first give respect and show love before expecting to receive it back from their people. Leaders must *earn* their title. In the words of Craig Groeschel, "people will follow a leader with a heart faster than a leader with a title."[5]

How many business leaders see themselves as if they are in a separate class from so-called ordinary people? They demand special perks, have separate bathrooms, ride different elevators, you name it. Great leaders are humble. In the times of Jesus, the mode of transportation for most people was to walk. Wearing sandals in a sandy and arid climate, the feet of travelers quickly became sweaty and dirty. What did Jesus do? He showed his closest followers how to lead with humility by washing their feet. How many leaders in this day and age would go to such lengths to show their love through such an act?

There's another great example of humility that Scott

follows, and that standard was set by his CEO, Rodney Garner. Scott told me a story of how their President and CEO, Rodney Garner, was on an airplane with his wife when he was approached by a few girls from a local high school. Rodney, being the friendly guy he is, recognized the girls and started up a conversation with them. In the course of the conversation, the girls asked, "hey, do you work at Mountain Alarm?"

"I do," Rodney replied.

"Oh so do you work for Boyd Ferrin?"

"I do," he again replied.

At the time, Boyd Ferrin was one of Mountain Alarm's sales guys. This may not sound like a huge display of humility, but it is! How many CEOs would have said yes when asked if they worked for someone several layers under them in their organization? How many would have stuck out their chest saying, actually I own that company, he works for me, or something similar? This wasn't the case with Rodney. Even outside of work, Rodney lived the principles that he established in his business by putting his people first. If I had to guess, in Rodney's mind he does work for Boyd and every other person who gives their all for his company. All leaders should take note of this attitude and model it if they want to be considered *great* by those around them.

CHAPTER 2

GREAT LEADERS ALWAYS FOLLOW VISION

No great CEO has ever said, "Our vision is to make a lot of money." Great CEOs are driven by a guiding vision to make or do something great for others. Take the example from before of Microsoft. Bill Gates had a vision of democratizing the ownership of PCs so that every person could benefit.

Have you ever talked to a CEO who couldn't tell you their vision for their organization? Lack of direction and vision in one of the most significant factors in creating disengaged employees, wasted efforts, and failing companies. If a leader intends to be great, they must first give their people a guiding vision that will allow the organization to continue long after the founder is gone. If there is no vision that you or your team are basing decisions off of and striving toward fulfilling, then you will likely never accomplish anything worthy of being called great.

For a leader to *lead*, the organization must *follow* and know what it is that they are following. Without a vision to guide decisions, how do you expect your people to be engaged on the right activities, if they are taking any action at all?

Have you ever talked to middle managers, front-line managers, or individual contributors who couldn't articulate their organization's vision? Just as important as it is for the CEO and his or her staff to have a vision for their organization, it is equally as important that they communicate that vision repeatedly, so the vision becomes ingrained deep within the organization. There's a whole separate topic about how and how often to communicate vision, but the first two steps are foundational: 1) have a vision to follow and 2) make sure your people know, understand, and internalize that vision.

Importance of Vision - Purpose

What is it that gets you out of bed to work every morning? If your answer is anything short of the purpose behind your company's vision, then the efforts you give will never be as optimal as they could be. If your organization is filled with individuals, from top to bottom, who knew, internalized, and strove toward the organization's vision, every day, then there would be nothing stopping you.

We all need purpose in life. Pastor and Author, Rick Warren, saw how true this was when his book, *The Purpose Driven Life*, sold many more copies than he could have ever imagined. Why did his book do so well? Why is Simon Sinek's work so popular in his book, *Start With Why*? The answer is simple. We all want to know what it is we are here for, and while we are here, we want to know what it is that we should be doing for fulfillment.

Today's organization, whether private, public, non-profit, or church group has the opportunity to fill the lives of its members with the purpose and fulfillment we all seek as human beings. If only the CEO and his or her staff knows what the vision is, the likelihood of that vision ever being reached is not high. A vision that is created to just check a box or to have something to hang on the wall of boardrooms is a vision that will hold no water. However, a vision that is real, meaningful, and hungrily sought after by the entire organization, is a vision that will change the lives of people inside and outside of that organization.

Do you want a streamlined way to determine employee fit? Do you want a way to increase employee engagement? How about employee turnover? Many of the everyday problems faced by managers would not exist, or at least be dramatically reduced, if we would simply cast the vision for our people. It's not that it is hard to do, but it does take time, commitment, and passion. If you, regardless of where you sit in the hierarchy, are not passionate about how the purpose your role fits into the larger picture of the organization and the way your role helps the organization get a few steps closer to reaching its vision, how do you expect anyone around you to be?

Passion is contagious and passionate people quickly realize who does not belong on the team. And for managers, who are responsible for instilling vision and purpose within others, it is exponentially important that you are passionate and that you give purpose to your people. The days of answering hard questions with "be happy you have a job" (yes, I've heard this said to employees) are long over. Give someone purpose, something to be passionate about, and you will quickly see the mindset of your people change from "doing a job" toward "accomplishing a mission."

Importance of Vision - Direction

David Ng, CEO of GoGame and former CEO of Gumi Asia, says, "Leading a company is like rowing a boat... if everyone in the organization is rowing in different directions, you will end up stuck in one place, even after a lot of rowing." Great leaders are intentional and focused in their efforts, and great organizations follow their leader with equally intense focus. Without a clear vision, how can your people be focused and rowing in the same direction?

As an organization grows, it is even more critical to not only provide direction but to continually reinforce that direction. Through your vision, your organization will be enabled to grow without losing focus. Lack of clarity and perceived lack of purpose are two powerfully negative forces that will drive members of your organization to disengage or start rowing in the wrong direction (and possibly intentionally). It is even more common for this to happen when the organization scales and you are no longer able to directly provide the direction and vision for the organization to each new team member. The larger your company grows, the more critical it becomes to ensure that your vision is consistently reinforced at each level of your organization.

Another force fighting against the alignment of focus and direction is silos. The concept of silos creating communication gaps has been discussed at length in the literary works of others, but it is also important to realize the impact that silos have on the ability for an organization to stay aligned on mission, purpose, and direction. David Ng told me of a recent story where silos caused a gap in a product release, and there was rework and long hours needed to remediate the problem. Because two of his product teams, working on separate parts of the game, were not aligned in their efforts and focused on the direction of the overall product, the release of the game would have been catastrophic. If the error had not been found, there would have been no way for customers to make payments, the developers would not have been able to collect revenues, and the customers would have had a terrible first impression with the new game. When divisions or teams lose sight of the organization's direction for the sake of their own key performance indicators, this sort of misalignment is bound to happen. In both stages of planning and execution, each team needs to ensure the alignment with the organization's direction.

David's company, GoGame, is a mobile game publisher out of Singapore whose vision is: "make good games great." David's vision is to let independent software vendors create outstanding games and lean on the expertise of David and his organization to ensure that the published product is great. The success of a mobile application launch is determined by a few, key factors, and GoGame offers the expertise to best position games to see success in the Southeast Asian market.

One way that David drives directional alignment around

his vision is to have every one of the two-hundred people in his organization play the games before they are published. Every person from marketing, to customer service, to finance will be issued a challenge to see who can reach a certain level the fastest and accomplish a certain number of tasks within the game. Every person is immersed in the game their company is working to make great.

Not only is it a great perk of working for a mobile game publisher, to get paid for playing games at work, but it is a powerful feedback mechanism for the company to compile a diverse set of inputs from two hundred people on what they like, don't like, and so on. Before going to market, each one of the two-hundred people in David's organization has the opportunity to be part of what makes that game great. What a great way to break down silos, encourage collaboration, and align efforts around vision. Are there creative ways that you can influence your organization, division, or team to align better with the direction that leads them all toward the vision?

Importance of Vision - Succession Planning

With little exception, if an organization makes a hire from outside of their organization, then there is clear indication of the organization's leaders failing to do their jobs. One of the top priorities of leaders is developing other leaders as successors. Hiring from outside of the organization means you have failed on one of two levels. The first is that you failed to develop your people. The second is you hired the wrong people. Either way, it is *your* fault if you have to find your successor from outside of *your* organization.

There are many stories of great company founders who see their organizations tank upon their departure. On two notable occasions, founders have had to return to the organizations to "get the train back on the tracks," so to speak. One of the examples is Howard Schultz of Starbucks. Although he was not the founder, Schultz made Starbucks into the company we know today. Starbucks, under Schultz, had obtained a significant level of success. He grew the company to a national chain and led Starbucks to international success. When he left in 2000, what happened? Things started changing in the Starbucks stores under new CEO Jim Donald, and the customers did not respond well. Why did this happen? Either Schultz did not instill in Jim his vision for Starbucks, or Jim deviated from the vision. It was not even that Jim was hired from the outside. Before becoming CEO, Jim was serving as President of the North American Division of Starbucks.[1] Though coming from inside the organization, the vision for Starbucks, the very core of what made Starbucks what everyone loved, was no longer a reality. Jim was asked to step down as a result.

The first decision Schultz made upon his return was to explicitly communicate the vision that he had for Starbucks and reinstate the "distinctive Starbucks experience." Schultz succeeded in his efforts, and Starbucks returned to the premier coffee shop with an atmosphere that, once again, everyone loves. Now that Kevin Johnson has come on as President and CEO of Starbucks, time will tell whether or not the original vision of the company will remain intact and if the "distinctive Starbucks experience" will continue as initially envisioned.

Although Schultz had to learn from his prior mistake, there are examples of great leaders who do successfully pass down their vision to the next generation of leaders, and Mary Kay is a great example.

Mary Kay Ash was a leader who succeeded in passing along her vision to those who would eventually be responsible for the long-term viability of her company, Mary Kay Cosmetics. Mary Kay wanted nothing more than to work for a company who treated others as they wanted to be treated. She felt that the Golden Rule would allow for customers, employees, and the organization to all benefit. She dreamed of the day when a woman would be able to fully utilize her skills and talents and be compensated equally to their male counterparts. In that dream, women would not be limited by any proverbial "ceilings," and they would be able to reach any goal that they were smart enough and dedicated enough to reach.

Up until 1963, when Mary Kay Cosmetics started, it was almost unheard of for women to be business owners or making much more than their husbands. There were times where women made so much money with Mary Kay Cosmetics that their husbands were able to quit jobs they hated for lower paying jobs they loved.

Customers were given facials and taught how to optimally use the beauty products to enhance their looks and therefore their confidence. Mary Kay was a firm believer that if a woman looked good, they would feel good. She also believed that it was this confidence that enabled women to do much more than they ever before thought possible.

Mary Kay's organization has and continues to see her vision being carried out across the globe. It was the enthusiasm of her vision that attracted so many talented women in the early years, and it was her enthusiasm that gave the organization its early successes even when facing adversity and trials. When you articulate a clear vision that is attached to a higher purpose than making money, people buy into that and loyalty, commitment, and passion follow.

It has been over half a century since the founding of Mary Kay Cosmetics, and the vision Mary Kay had for her company has not changed. Although Mary Kay passed away in 2001, the organization lives on and is still thriving. The company continues to operate on the Golden Rule, and Mary Kay Cosmetics continues to strive to enrich the lives of the consultants, their consultant's families, and their customers.

Why was Mary Kay so successful at establishing such a strong vision and a company that continued after her when others like Steve Jobs and Howard Schultz were not? It comes down to what we'll talk about at length, later on, communication. Mary Kay was a master communicator, enthusiastically sharing her vision and her passion with everyone. People joined her organization because they believed in her, and they were inspired by her vision. When you give someone something to believe in, a purpose in life, you don't have to motivate them. *Commitment to a vision* garners motivation and buy-in, not pep rallies, catchy slogans, or charismatic speeches.

Great leaders cannot be successful without a successor, and the successor needs to understand and be able to continue carrying out the organization's vision. Mary Kay created many extensions of herself. She instilled her vision with *every* Director and National Sales Director as they were going through their promotion training. Understanding Mary Kay's vision enabled her Directors to pass it on to their Consultants who passed it on to their Consultants when they too moved up the "Ladder of Success." Mary Kay's commitment to enriching the lives of her people and growing an experienced management team is the very reason why she succeeded in developing successors while others have not. Part of developing a robust and professional management "bench" is having and instilling your vision so that once you're gone, your vision will live on.

CHAPTER 3

GREAT LEADERS ALWAYS FOLLOW INDICATORS

There's a difference between following indicators and following trends. Which is better will depend on what you're trying to accomplish as an organization. The difference comes down to adapting to a changing environment (trends) vs. an intentional push toward an opportunity based on insights gleaned by following indicators. Regardless of what you're looking at when it comes to trends versus indicators, following a trend typically means that you're late. Whether you are considering the viability of your business model, cultural indicators that point to organizational health, indicators of poor results based on early performance, or any number of others, the point of following indicators rather than trends is that you always want to be ahead of opportunities and threats, when possible.

Connecting Dots

The number of dots waiting to be connecting in this world is endless. In the words of Steve Jobs, "You can't connect the dots looking forward; you can only connect them looking backward. So you have to trust that the dots will somehow connect in your future. You have to trust in something - your gut, destiny, life, karma, whatever. This approach has never let me down, and it has made all the difference in my life."[1]

I've heard it said that there's no such thing as a true invention but there are a series of dots that get connected to piece existing materials together for a new, productive use. That's what innovation is, seeing what others miss and piecing together a solution of unique value that, today, does not exist.

One of the dots that is often overlooked is when a business model innovation takes place in an industry adjacent to yours. Great leaders are always thinking, always aggregating information and ideas. To be competitively sound, you must ask yourself how shifts in the macro-environment could potentially affect your specific industry or business model.

For example, when the internet became ubiquitous, how many retail companies understood this to be a "dot" that could impact their business? By the vast number of retail companies scaling back physical locations or going out of business completely, it is clear that many executives did not have a broad enough mindset toward this technological shift and how it would potentially affect consumer behavior. Even after Amazon proved their online retail success with online book sales, there were still too many companies who did not find it relevant to them. Today, they are paying for it with lost jobs, lost revenue, lost market share, and diminished legacies.

Indicators Kill Best Practices

Companies that build their strategies on "best practices" seem to always be in a mode of catching up to those they imitate. Michael Porter, the "father of strategy," has a couple of things to say about best practice strategy. - "If all you're trying to do is essentially the same thing as your rivals, then it's unlikely that you'll be very successful." He also says, "Strategy is about *setting yourself apart* from the competition. It's not a matter of being better at what you do - it's a matter of being different at what you do."[2] Michael Porter taught what great leaders know, to do something great, you must offer a unique value to your customers. As a leader, you are playing it safe, void of creativity, and not actually leading if all your "strategy" consists of is mirroring the activities of other organizations.

Who determines what a "best practice" is anyway? If most companies follow a best practice strategy, then there is simply an industry imitating the first company which showed some signs of success. But what if their practices are not "best?" The very phrase, "best practice," sounds close-minded and void of innovation. If something is "best," why improve it or attempt to disrupt it? Rex Rollo, Chief Financial Officer of America First Credit Union, told me, "best practices are not always best practices. And that's up to who? A lot of times that is up to folks who haven't been down in the trenches, and I think that any leader needs to get down in the trenches with the people; you have to listen to what they are saying."

There's only one reason why leaders should care about what industry calls a best practice: Innovation. When great leaders enter a new environment, it *is* important to understand what the "best practices" are. Whether you are entering a new industry or a new job role, you want to identify the methods which are working well. The question that great leaders ask is, Should they *still* be (or ever have been) considered best? Great leaders identify the industry standard, or best practices, for the sole purpose of figuring out how to set a *new* standard. They ask questions like, "how can this be better?" or "what is wrong with the practice that no one has addressed yet?" "What are the customers saying?" "How can I disrupt it?" Great leaders do not simply identify the "best practices" to imitate them. No, you identify them and make them better so that the new best practice comes from you. You assess them so you can set and continually reset what that best practice is. By doing this, great leaders position themselves to lead their organizations and their organizations to lead its industry.

Rex shared with me a story about how following indicators allowed him to see past his industry's best practices to make the best choice, given the situation. He shared with me how he started his leadership journey in the early 90s, in the Savings and Loans business, by turning around his company. In the late 80s to early 90s, the Savings and Loans industry was going under, primarily due to unstable lending in real estate. The way Rex was able to save the nonprofit Savings and Loan Company was to re-capitalize it through venture funding and turn it into a Savings Bank. This decision allowed the company to survive a highly turbulent time in that industry.

When the financial crisis of 2008 hit, Rex had already

made the decision, two years prior, not to repeat the mistakes made by most in the Savings and Loan industry back in the early 90s. Rex had already seen the effects that a crashing real estate market would have on financial institutions, and he saw that same crash starting again in the early parts of 2006. The real indicator in 2006, like in the early 90s, was the inflation of homes.

Rex was in the Savings and Loans business for nineteen years before he saw the inflation of homes blowing up in the early 90s. He was no novice to the industry, and he knew things were off. He remarked about how it does not make financial sense that homes would be selling for more than the cost to build them. There must have been an issue with the market, and there was. This was the indicator that had Rex scratching his head in the 90s, and it was the same indicator that made Rex resolute about his position in 2006 through the Great Recession.

Luckily, Rex was CFO in 2006, and that position gave him the power to make the decisions necessary to weather another financial crisis. That decision in 2006 was to guide America First away from real estate, long before the collapse in 2008 hit. Rex credits this recognition of indicators to experience. He lived through times of adversity, and he was able to navigate turbulent waters with the wisdom that came from his experience. Because of this experience, he was able to take much swifter action on those indicators once he saw them again. George Santayana once said, "Those who cannot remember the past are condemned to repeat it."[3] Rex would agree, and he was also one who would prove the opposite to be true. He did remember the past, and he was able to capitalize on the opportunity presented to him due to this foresight.

So what exactly did America First, under Rex Rollo's guidance, do to be successful when so many financial institutions were weakened or crippled during the same period? Rex told me there were two primary things. The first was that the Credit Union worked with their customers. In the Savings and Loan crisis, everyone panicked. The Savings and Loan institutions took back homes from people and tried to resell them in a distressed market. The model didn't work, so Rex had America First act differently. America First worked with their customers to keep their homes. These customers then stayed with America First and became incredibly loyal customers.

The second thing America First did was that it did not panic under the weight of the pressure from regulators. The regulators were advising all the financial institutions to dump their real estate loans all at once. Well, America First had been going away from Real Estate for two years already, so the number of loans they had was minimal in comparison to others in the industry. Even so, America First did not dump all of their loans, going against the "best practice" of the time. Rex knew, as he saw in the 90s, that the market would come back.

America First was not finished breaking trends and going against the best practices of its industry. Many financial institutions went under during the great recession of 2008, and many of them were selling out to try to recoup anything they could. Rex saw this as a growth opportunity in the long term. In a time where financial institutions were selling off everything, Rex and America first decided to start acquiring some of the failed banks. Why? The economy was so bad that the failed banks were selling at fifty cents on the dollar. In the short-term, the investments looked crazy, knowing these failed institutions would not be profitable for a few years. In the long-term; however, these investments would lead to significant growth for America First.

In Weber County, Utah, where the America First's headquarters resides, growth was minimal year over year. Rex knew that to see growth, there would need to be expanded reach. In a credit union, you cannot be a member anywhere you want though. To be a member, you have to live within the "field of membership," as Rex explained it. Well, with every acquired credit union, that field of membership expands, and so does the growth of the credit union.

The first credit union acquired was in Clark County, Nevada. The credit union there was in dire straits, and the regulator paid America First to take them over. With this acquisition, America First's field of membership would now encompass all of Clark County. This gave America First access to the entire Las Vegas customer base, as well as a large surrounding area in southern Nevada. Many in the industry asked America First questions like, "You bought a negative company in negative times? That doesn't make any sense." As Rex puts it, "if you keep a clear head...you can go in and buy things very cheaply." Rex, being the CFO, understands finance and math. But you do not need to be a CFO to know that a negative multiplied by a negative equals a positive. That's the math Rex did, and that is how he helped America First substantially grow their business.

Leading Up

The insight of a potential opportunity often comes within the organization from those who are great at connecting the dots or have insights which their superiors have missed. Those dots, in this case, are indicators that surround a market and are waiting to be put together to create unique value. That is how innovation happens. In his book, *Only the Paranoid Survive*, Andy Grove, Co-Founder and CEO of Intel Corporation, argues that it's often the C-Suite who doesn't notice trends until it's too late.[4]

This unfortunate truth of Senior and Executive management missing *trends* makes Senior Leaders even more prone to overlook *indicators*. In Nina Bowman's HBR article, *4 Ways to Improve Your Strategic Thinking Skills*, she argues that strategic thinking is not only the responsibility of the C-Suite.[5] She states that it's an imperative to be a strategic thinker at all levels of an organization. Great leaders are humble enough to accept this and allow others within their organization to lead up and influence their decisions. To get ahead of the trends, Senior Management needs to be communicating with the front-line leaders who recognize these indicators of opportunity, vet them according to their vision, synthesize the feedback into strategy, and allow their organization to execute.

If you are not the CEO, it is imperative you learn how to lead up and start looking for opportunities to do it. What determines how far you move up tomorrow will be how well you lead up today.[6] Opportunities will present themselves when you see something that your superior(s) have missed, overlooked, or otherwise disregarded. Although you are not the leader of the organization, it *is* your responsibility to be a leader within the organization. You must take that responsibility seriously and act on the indicators you see. That action may come in the form of leveraging what, if any, power you do have within the organization, or it might take a series of meetings eventually leading to a meeting with the decision maker in your organization.

Once you have the attention of your superiors, it is still critical that you present the information correctly. There is a level of due diligence that is needed, and you'll need to make sure you can articulate what the indicators are, how they connect, and what impact they could potentially have on the organization. From there, it is up to your senior leaders to act, but you will have done your job. As a friend of mine once said, "If everyone does their job, the job gets done."

Feedback loops are necessary for any organization to maximize its effectiveness. In the words of Craig Groeschel, "No organization will ever be what it could be without honest, upward communication."[7] Top-level management *needs* to be receiving feedback and input from the front lines to make informed decisions. Great leaders know that to be a great leader, you must develop other great leaders. If your executive leadership team is doing their job of developing other great leaders and that trend of leadership development cascades down, deep into the organization, then you will do yourself no favors by making decisions in the silos of an executive staff meeting. It would be a waste of valuable resources to not consider the inputs of your people, especially if you've hired and developed the right talent.

On the other side of the coin, it's not the responsibility of the executive leadership team to go out and solicit strategic feedback from the rest of their organization. It is the responsibility of leaders within the organization to stand up, step out, and speak up when they see something. It can be indicators of opportunities or indicators of threats. Either way what you see could make a positive or negative impact on the organization. It *is* your responsibility to speak up. If this feedback is not consistently making its way up the chain of leadership, decision making and performance will never achieve optimal results.

It's all too tempting to be caught thinking that your senior leaders should see what you see and know what you know. This is hardly ever the case, and this is why and where you bring value to the organization as a leader within the organization.

I would be remiss if I did not give a word of caution in your attempts to lead up. If your communication approach with your superiors has a tone of condescension, then you probably won't get very far, and the looming indicators will likely never get addressed. Regardless the situation, regardless the feedback or response you get, and regardless how right you know you are, there must always be a tone of honor and respect when leading up. Being firm in stating your case will be necessary, but you must have the humility to honor your superiors, even if you feel that they are making a poor decision. It's your job is to raise awareness; it is their job to make the decision.

Not to be repetitive, but you want to ensure that your attitude is appropriate while communicating your insights.

Self-ambition should never be the driving motivation. As we've said before, great leaders are fueled by intrinsic motivators. This is what drives them to make an impact on and drive value for their organization. As one of the great leaders in American history, John F. Kennedy, said in his inaugural address, "My fellow Americans, ask not what your country can do for you, ask what you can do for your country."[8] Great leaders within organizations ask that same question of themselves. The ambition and drive comes from wanting to see your organization thrive and grow. As a byproduct of this desire, you will likely thrive and grow as well, but it is not the basis of why great leaders lead up.

Pain Points

Great leaders see problems, or pain points, as opportunities. David Ng says, "The messier it is, the more opportunity there is to create… the more chaos, the more opportunity to create." David knows what all great leaders know, pain points are a clear indicator of opportunity.

For example, David Ng described how the Japanese Gaming market experiences a tremendous pain point when it comes to publishing new game titles. The expertise, language skills, and resources to take a decent Japanese game successfully to a global market is incredibly rare to find. The Japanese game developers end up becoming hindered from becoming as successful as they potentially could be. When you look at the numbers, around ninety percent of the Japanese game developers only market to the Japanese market. They do not even attempt to penetrate markets outside of their home country.

Where David's company, GoGame, becomes extremely valuable to this market is through the expertise that he and his team bring to address that pain point. GoGame has all of the publishing services, like localization, needed to address the global market. Game developers in Japan can focus their efforts on making good games, and GoGame focuses on making the games great and a global success.

GoGame goes a step further by creating additional products to address pain points of the emerging markets in Southeast Asia. An example of this would be GoGame's product, GoPay. David knows that in emerging countries, about ninety-three percent of people do not own credit cards, so they cannot make payments through the mainstream stores. GoPay gives these customers an alternative payment channel which allows his clients to reach an untapped audience of potential customers.

When a great leader identifies pain points in their culture, their industry, their business, or even their product, there is ample opportunity for growth around a unique value proposition. What pain points have you noticed in your culture, your industry, your business, or your product? Where can you offer unique value to your customers?

Organizational Culture

Culture is a topic that is given much attention and rightfully so. There are many opinions on what constitutes a healthy culture, and there is a range of types of cultures that are, in fact, healthy. There's not a one size fits all solution to building or maintaining a healthy work environment, but there are indeed warning signs or indicators of a culture that is becoming unhealthy. These indicators are of much higher importance to leaders if we want sustained success for our organizations. It's vital to the longevity of an organization to establish the culture that you want to see and that fits with your business. It's equally as necessary to maintain that culture.

To maintain a healthy culture you will want to look for indicators of unhealthy behaviors and ensure that individuals in your organization are not bringing values into the environment that are contrary to the values you wish to see present.

The 5 C's

I learned about the 5 "C's" of an unhealthy culture from Scott Sessions. He share this with me as he reflected on common issues that leaders face during mergers and acquisitions. Mergers and acquisitions can look favorable for a number of reasons. It could be an effort to find synergies through vertical integration. Other times, leaders might feel an acquisition could buy them time with Wall Street and offset the recent poor performance. Unfortunately, cultural alignment between the two organizations is often only an afterthought. But like when you forget your coat on a cold day, you quickly notice the problem as soon as you walk out of the door. Indeed, this was the case when Mountain Alarm made their largest acquisition to date.

Mountain Alarm's culture is one of love, respect, collaboration, and loyalty. Love is a proven tenant of their culture by the tenure of their employees. From the leadership team to the hands-on technicians, it is more common than not to find individuals who enjoy the majority of their career with the company. This is a rarity for most organizations today. When the acquisition of Kenco was taking place, Scott and the leadership team quickly noticed that Kenco's culture was very much opposite of what Mountain Alarm had established and expected. The 5 "C's" were very much alive in this organization. The 5 "C's" are Command, Control, Criticize, Compel, and Compare. I'll take the liberty of adding a sixth "C" which is another indicator of poor culture, *complaining*.

Command and Control

Employees *hate* micromanagement. In a command and control environment, your people will suffocate due to the lack of latitude given to them. No one likes to hear, "because I'm your manager" or "because I said so." Even as a child, we hated hearing "because I said so." When you take the time to explain *why* you "said so," you show that you care. You show you have a valid reason for why you said what you said, and it builds trust. Like I'll talk about more in chapter six, you'll never build an organization that lasts beyond you if you are not communicating the right things and communicating them consistently.

Criticism

With all of the books and articles in the world on how to motivate employees, there are much fewer on what actions to avoid if you intend to *keep* motivated employees. Without a doubt, criticism is one of the fastest ways to demotivate an employee.

Unfortunately, semantics play in role in many manager's understanding of this concept. Some managers confuse criticism for coaching. Similar to a command and control leadership culture, a culture that employs the tactic of criticism does the opposite of show love to your people. In any aspect of life, people will not follow someone who they do not feel has their best interest at heart. People will not support someone who belittles them.

Allow me to make clear another point about criticism, and we've all been guilty of this at one point or another. Putting on a facade in front of your people and then criticizing them in front of your peers or superiors, behind closed doors, is *not* acceptable. A leader's job is to develop other leaders. How can you grow others to be leaders if you're tearing them down behind closed doors? And what message does this send to your peers and superiors? If your employees, peers, or superiors know that you frequently criticize people behind their backs, then what do those people think you're saying about them when they're not in the room?

Great leaders show humility. Great leaders don't talk down to or about other people. Great leaders don't turn a blind eye to poor performance or misbehavior; they do something about it. They coach their people to become better, and they're compassionately honest with their people when there are gaps in performance or behavior. Regardless of the situation, great leaders have the best interest of their people in mind. If there are performance or behavioral issues that are persistent, then we identify whether the problem lies in a positional or organizational fit or if the attitudes and values of the individual are not a fit. Great leaders *never* change the culture to fit the people. Great leaders identify what culture *they* want for their organization and they hire and fire based on that cultural fit. Either way, the issue lies with the leader. Great leaders never criticize. Great leaders empathize, organize, and mobilize.

Compel

There's not one person who would say they loved being forced to do something. Even if the thing you are being forced to do is something you would typically like doing, the fact that someone is attempting to force you to do it will put a sour taste in your mouth.

As leaders, we want to ensure that we're hiring people who are the right fit for the organization and the role. If a person is in an environment where their talents are utilized, they are growing, and they fit in with the culture, you will probably never have to worry about forcing or compelling that person to do anything. That motivation will naturally come as a byproduct of someone in a position they love, utilizing their talents, and working for an organization where they can grow.

Great leaders do not treat their people like children. We may try to force our children to eat their vegetables, but adults should not have to be forced to do things, because they are adults. If someone doesn't want to work, they don't have to. They might not have a job very long, but that is their choice. Wasting time and effort to compel those who don't want to work, to work, will take much of your emotional and physical stamina. This takes away from those who should be getting the attention. It will drag the team down and will stagnate progress of the organization. Organizations seeing leaders who try to manage by compulsion either have the wrong leader or the wrong people. Either way, the presence of a compulsive atmosphere is an indicator of a problem that will hinder you from having or keeping the organizational culture, and performance, you want to maintain.

Compare

If you're a parent, then you'll notice the parallels in parenting multiple children. God did not create any two people the same. Even with identical twins, no two people are exactly alike. As every fingerprint is distinctly different from any other, every human being is different from every other human on the planet. Of course, there will be similarities, but we cannot make the mistake of comparing people to one another. There is nothing more divisive.

The topic of diversity, and the benefits diversity has on teams, has been trending for several years. There is the topic of surface-level diversity like with gender, race, and age. Then there are the subsurface factors of diversity that deal with how people think. With all of the studies which prove the benefits of having a diverse team, why would we be crazy enough to continue in our comparisons of the unique individuals on that team? In a command and control environment, you might want everyone following your orders, your way, when you say. In a healthy environment, you'll feed off of the diversity, allow your people to leverage their unique talents, and enjoy the fruits of your team's synergy.

Do not compare. Instead, you need to enable your people to bring their whole selves to work and use their unique talents to their fullest potential. It is your role to bring out your people's abilities to their fullest and ensure alignment of activities and objective to get the right results.

Complain

Great leaders are not complainers. Complaining looks outward and points the finger. Complaining is a void of ownership and is the opposite behavior of a leader. Nothing fires me up more than to hear a manager complaining about one of their direct reports. You hired them! Stop whining and coach them, help them, and encourage them. Do something more productive than complaining about them, because it helps no one. If team members are complaining about each other, then there is an issue. It might be a lack of trust amongst one another, or it could be that some team members are not showing the expected level of accountability. Regardless of the reason behind the complaining, if complaining exists in your organization or on your team, there is a real problem that needs fixing. You might have hired the wrong people. You might have not enabled your people to act with autonomy, so they feel helpless. Either way, solving this problem starts with you, the leader.

CHAPTER 4

GREAT LEADERS ALWAYS FOLLOW THEIR GUT

How many decisions do leaders have to make with limited data and facts? Leaders get their positions because of their ability to think strategically and make decisions. As leaders progress in their careers, earning higher positions of authority and influence, there is a track record built of following their intuitions and making decisions. Does this mean that their choices are flawless? Of course not. It is the failures that help humble leaders further refine their decision-making skills. Even great leaders will falter in decision making at times, so where do the issues come from?

Issues in Decision Making

The first issue comes in when leaders let pride rule their decisions. How many times have you seen leaders make decisions only to realize that they're poor decisions? This is not uncommon, but the issue comes in when they fail to change course due to pride. It is hard to swallow sunk costs when so much has been invested into a bad idea, but again, it is pride and fear of looking incompetent that allow leaders to continually throw resources at a bad idea. The key is to fail often, early, and cheap (if possible), so that sunk costs are low. And it is more comfortable to back out of smaller investments. Even when the data screams that a decision can't fail, it's best to start with a small-scale effort and grow from success rather than go all in on an initiative that could lead to a devastating loss.

The second issue is being too reliant on data. If I learned one thing in statistics, it's the fact that statistics can be made to say whatever you want them to. Statistics might show outdated trends with no indication of what will happen tomorrow. All collected data is past information and not a guarantee of the future. Just ask Wall Street when the markets crashed into recessions. Regardless of the upward trends, crashes happen. Disruption happens. Things change. Don't get me wrong, data is undoubtedly useful, and looking at trends, both internally and externally, is necessary. But the point is that an over-reliance on data to make decisions is a mistake. Being cognizant of indicators can help companies to avoid being disrupted or weakened by a rapid change that data couldn't predict (at least until deep learning takes over).

The third issue stems from the second. When there is an over-reliance on data, what happens when a leader faces situations where they have to make a big decision with little to no data? Do they wait until data becomes available? I've heard it said, and I agree with the statement, that sometimes an average decision made quickly is better than a great decision made too late. Buba Turner advises, "In the absence of data, make a decision and start collecting that data right away." Once you start collecting the data, then you can better understand if you made the right choice, if minor adjustments are needed, or if you need to move in an entirely different direction.

It works the same with feedback. The longer you wait for beta testing or releasing new products, the longer it takes to get feedback on it. The alternative is to iteratively design, prototype, and user-test your product (or service) through the development cycle. If you had an iteration every month, which was user-tested, then you could have much quicker feedback cycles and make adjustments in a more timely manner.

Going back to decision making, we live in turbulent and disruptive times. Leaders will often find themselves wondering what move they should make and understandably second-guessing themselves. The key to success in the 21st Century will be quick, informed decisions which are iterative through a process of learning and adjustments.

When great leaders dare to decide, they give their organizations the opportunity to fail early, fail cheap, and make adjustments along the way. Leaders who wait until the data is available might be late to the party, have to act quickly to catch up, and better have chosen the right path. If not, you risk significant investments, with little time to adjust, and failure will be costly.

Seizing Opportunities

David Ng states, "Your gut always comes first, then due diligence." David's first business was a computer business that he started from the ground up. He built and grew his brand and received attention from firms in Japan. From the word of these Japanese customers, Russians began to take notice of the work David's small company was doing. When the Russians made a surprise trip to Singapore to offer their services as a hardware distributor, David was unaware of the connection with his Japanese customer. He found that out later.

When the towering Russian came into David's office, he did not speak a bit of English and had a translator to help facilitate the conversation. On the surface, David had no clue how the Russian firm knew anything about his company and wanted nothing to do with a deal that seemed to be incredibly sketchy. However, as a believer in fate, David's gut told him to explore the opportunity. He decided to give these gentlemen his time, hear them out, and do some due diligence to see if there was an opportunity in what they were proposing. He figured that if they flew all of those miles from Russia to Singapore to meet with him, he owed them at least that much. As the conversation progressed, David began to think this proposed partnership could be a massive opportunity for him.

It turns out that the distribution partnership with the Russian firm was a significant opportunity and started David on a whirlwind of ensuing successes. The next would come when he received a call from his distributor in Taiwan.

In this conversation, David was introduced to the owner of Linksys USA. The owner of Linksys wanted to go global, and he had heard of the success and strong reputation David had earned in the Asian market. What he wanted was for David to help him take Linksys global and "conquer the world," as David put it.

David asked him, "When would you like to start?"

"Tomorrow," the gentleman replied.

"Where?" David continued.

"Japan."

David jumped on a plane the next day. Writing the business plan on the flight, David flew to Japan and met with the Linksys USA owner in the city of Akihabara. They met in a small room, spent six hours talking, and in that room the decision was made to launch Linksys Asia. They went on to be incredibly successful and the market leader in home routers for much of the 1990s. Linksys Asia was built into a billion-dollar company and later sold to Cisco in 2003.

What David was able to accomplish, going from a one-man shop in Singapore selling networking hardware to running Linksys Asia, would be considered, by anyone, a huge success. And every other success that followed with SEGA, Gumi, and now GoGame can be attributed to the fact that David followed his gut one time in his office, with a couple of Russian gentlemen who offered him a distribution partnership.

Even in the case of Linksys, David saw the opportunity and pursued the opportunity globalize the firm, with only a couple of days' notice and a six-hour conversation. David says that "the problem with leaders today is that there is too heavy of a reliance on data, analytics, and overly calculated decisions." For him, the gut is first. He asks himself two questions before pursuing opportunities. First, do I dare to do it? Second, do I believe I can do it? If both answers are yes, then he goes for it. Great leaders trust their instincts and are decisive when opportunities present itself. Nobody accomplishes anything great by shrinking back from or tiptoeing toward opportunity.

Investing From Your Gut

Another success story of following your gut in decision making comes from Scott Sessions and a significant investment decision that he made in 2010. An old friend of Scott's, Tim Snow, had approached Scott with an investment opportunity after being let go from his job. They said the layoff was due to being overpaid, and the company was trying to cut costs in the challenging economy.

Having a background starting companies and working for companies like Mountain Alarm, Tim felt he had a lot he could offer in adding a branch of Mountain Alarm in Phoenix, Arizona. At this time Mountain Alarm only had an excess cash flow of about $500,000. Scott, in his gut, knew this was the right investment to make and took the proposal to his partners. At Scott's recommendation and confidence in Tim, the venture launched in December 2010.

By April of 2011, the partners started to question whether or not this investment was wise and started asking if the whole thing should be shut down. Copper State Fire, the name of the Arizona branch, was sucking money and not seeing the desired performance. With these conversations happening behind the scenes, without Scott or Tim's knowledge, Scott was still prayerful that the business would turn around.

In his heart, Scott never felt uneasy about the decision to invest in Tim, and he had a gut feeling that it would be a profitable investment when things were said and done. The concerns were due to the lack of financial returns, but Scott felt at peace about how things would turn out. Meanwhile, the partners decided to extend the investment for a little while longer to see if it could get traction.

As it turns out, it was a great decision to invest in Copper State Fire, and it was a great decision by the partners to wait a little while for the results to show. Within six years, Copper State Fire went from three employees and no revenue to thirty-six employees and over $9,000,000 in annual revenue. Copper State Fire now represents almost 20% of Mountain Alarm's annual revenue.

At the beginning of it all, Tim told Scott that if he invested in Copper State Fire, he and the Mountain Alarm partners would look like Warren Buffett within five years. He was right, and Mountain Alarm has reaped the sweet reward of a great investment. But what made the investment great?

If Tim was in front of a group of venture capitalists, do you think they would have invested? It's likely that they would not have. Why? Tim had two prior failures in attempts of starting two similar businesses. Tim had no current customer-base in Phoenix, no partnerships for distribution, and no great data to share that could point to future success. So why did Scott champion the proposal and get the proposal approved by his partners? It goes back to the theme of this chapter: great leaders follow their gut. Scott knew Tim's character, and he didn't let past failures deter him from what would be a very prosperous future.

When I asked Scott why he invested, his answer was profound, "It was a gut feeling. We have three brains, a gut, a heart, and a brain. When it doesn't "feel right," it doesn't happen. We can try to make logical decisions like with the stock market or in dating relationships, but our gut will always lead us to the right conclusions."

Great leaders know when their intuitions are telling them something is right or wrong, and great leaders don't question that. There are countless stories like Scott and Tim's which point to this truth, and great leaders do not discount their intuition by only following data and hard numbers. Great leaders use data as a tool, but most companies today all have access to quality data. The thing that differentiates great leadership is being able to see beyond the numbers, trust their instincts, and follow their gut.

CHAPTER 5

GREAT LEADERS ALWAYS FOLLOW THROUGH

There are three major pillars of a great corporate culture: Discipline, Trust, and Accountability. Follow through is one factor that can add value to or destroy these three components, and that's why great leaders make a habit of always following through.

The three pillars of great corporate culture all complement one another. A culture of discipline allows for trust to be developed, because you know you're working with and for people and an organization who are focused in their efforts. Focus and discipline go hand in hand. I look at discipline in the form of a verb rather than a noun because I'm biased toward action. My favorite definition of discipline is "train oneself to do something in a controlled and habitual way."[1] The key here is that you are always doing something but in a controlled and habitual way.

When leaders discipline their actions, a couple of things happen. Discipline creates reliability and trust. In turn, discipline and trust garners the ever so desired buy-in from the very people we're trying to lead. Every leader knows that earning the confidence of your people is key to being a successful leader. And the act of disciplined behavior, decision making, and follow through are the foundational aspects of building that trust. There are many ways leaders are expected to follow through. Although it is not an exhaustive list, I want to share a few, fundamental examples of how you will be expected to follow through as a leader.

The Role Model

Every leader is a role model, whether good or bad. By default, the entire organization is watching you. Those outside of the organization, your communities, your shareholders, the media, and many others are watching you, whether you like it or not. Nothing can hide in the spotlight. Leaders have to be incredibly careful in what they say and do.

You can say something in passing, and someone can take that as firm direction. You might set expectations, only to break them in plain sight of the organization. Expectations create security. If your people do not know what to expect from you, there will be a shallow level of organizational security. The emotional security that comes from the consistency of your follow through is something that your organization cannot do without if it hopes to be great.

Following Through On Indicators

As we discussed in chapter three, great leaders always follow indicators. At times, you might be the *only* one who sees these indicators. Whether they are indicators of opportunities or indicators of threats, it is your responsibility to ensure these insights are communicated to your organization and followed through on.

In the example of Rex Rollo, CFO of America First, there were many times when he faced doubt from his peers and outsiders. There were many times when Rex would have to stand resolute in the face of the doubt and uncertainty which plagued those inside and outside of the organization. They did not know, see, or understand the indicators that Rex did. But as Rex said, "When you are in leadership, you must have the courage to *stick to it*."

One thing that happened to Rex is when the regulators came in and saw the acquisitions and assets that America First had and was gaining, they started asking questions. This was opposite of the best practice of the time which was to "sell while you can," like it was the end of all financial institutions forever. It sounds a bit dramatic, but this is what the trend in the industry was. Rex was constantly being pushed to sell off their assets, hearing crazy statements like, "your first loss is your best loss." Rex adamantly pushed back, and he was very passionate in telling me how necessary it was for him to have the resolve and stubbornness to say, "No. This is going to work; you have to believe me." Leaders, like Rex, will need this resolve to follow through on indicators, even when you might be the only person to see them.

Closing the Loop

As a leader, many people who rely on you for information, direction, and many other things. One of the things expected of you is to close the loop on open action items. As Buba Turner puts it, "What leaders tend to do is say, let me take that into account; let me follow up on that, but there is not the follow through that allows that person who brought up the issue to close the loop."

People need and want closure. This is true in many situations, and it is even more so in the context of leadership. Leaders can create a safe environment or an environment of chaos through their actions or inactions. In the case of closing the loop, if leaders fail to follow through on requests from their colleagues or employees, you leave people hanging and wondering how important they are to you. The last thing you need to do is have your people questioning how much you care about them.

Another thing that closing the loop does is create speed. When loops are left open, people will not be able to move forward on whatever it is they need closure on for their next step. On the flip side of that, when loops get closed it allows your people to move forward with clarity and confidence. There is always a direct correlation to speed. No direction equals slow or no movement. Or worse, movement in the wrong direction. Direction promotes action, and it gives your people the confidence to know their actions are not misplaced.

Values

A great example of a leader who has followed through on his stated values is Howard Schultz, former CEO of Starbucks. It is the philosophy of Schultz that success and growth will only come about when Starbucks can impact one cup of coffee, one customer, and one barista at a time. How has the former Starbucks' CEO followed up on his expressed beliefs?

How does Starbucks impact one cup of coffee? Starbucks has taken stance on being 100% "ethically sourced." To give credence to how Starbucks is attempting to follow through on their values, here's a section of their website* on how they ethically source their coffee, and the extension of the impact Starbucks looks to make:

> *We are committed to buying 100 percent ethically sourced coffee in partnership with Conservation International. To improve productivity and sustainability, we share our research and resources through our Farmer Support Centers—located in coffee-producing countries around the world. They're open to farmers regardless of whether they sell to us. Thanks to the support of our customers, we're also donating millions of disease-resistant trees to help farmers fight threats like coffee leaf rust. And through our Global Farmer Fund program, we're investing $50 million toward financing for farmers, allowing them to renovate their farm or pursue more sustainable practices.*[2]

How has Starbucks worked to impact one customer at a time? In my many visits to Starbucks, I have yet to meet an employee who was not upbeat and seemingly excited to be doing what they were doing. One day on my way to the airport, I stopped at a Starbucks a little after 4 AM. As a groggy customer who had not yet fully woken up, I would have fully understood a similar countenance from the barista who greeted me. Fortunately, this was not the case. I was impressed by the warm, energetic greeting. You would have thought it was mid-day, and the young lady was on her third cup of coffee. I was impressed. My day started with a smile, a burst of enthusiasm, and a caffeine-filled cup of goodness. It is in this way that Starbucks creates impact for their customers that goes beyond the cup of coffee.

Lastly, how does Starbucks follow through on its value of impacting each, individual barista? Starbucks has invested large sums of money in providing healthcare coverage for full-time and part-time employees. Likewise, Schultz, realizing the power of having an educated workforce and understanding the burden of college tuitions, has partnered with Arizona State University to offer several degree programs to their full and part-time employees at no cost. It's no wonder why Starbucks attracts and retains excellent employees, has an incredibly loyal customer base, and maintains an envied culture. When leaders prove their values by following through in their actions, it enables the type of success that Starbucks has enjoyed for many years.

Adversity

What happens when adversity hits? What happens when you're on the verge of losing everything? There are many forms of adversity, both inside and outside of your professional life. Even in the midst of turbulence, great leaders follow through on what they have set out to do.

Patrick Sutton, CEO of Auto FX Software, knows adversity as well as anyone. In 2009, Patrick heard that Auto FX Software, a photo effect and enhancements software company, was looking for someone to run marketing. Knowing the owner personally, he offered to fill that position. With his natural curiosity, interest in technology, and a knack for marketing, Patrick thought this would be a great opportunity.

Over time, the rest of the marketing staff was let go, and Patrick found himself with more and more responsibility. A large part of the overall business was being run directly by Patrick, and he saw a gap in the company. From its finances to its lack of investments back into the software, Auto FX was not doing what it needed to be a successful business. Much less, it was not doing anything to grow, innovate, or position itself to scale. After working a year for the Founder of Auto FX, Patrick saw an opportunity to purchase the company, revitalize it, and take it to new heights. At the time Patrick made the first offer, in 2010, Auto FX had already been in business and selling commercial licenses to large enterprise customers for over fifteen years.

It took several offers before the owner finally consented to negotiate a sale. Eventually, the owner relented, and Patrick got started on the due diligence before making the purchase. Part of the process included getting venture capital input on evaluating the company's worth. This venture capital firm, unfortunately, had more experience with manufacturing and other industries. They had little to no experience with software companies. With this lack of expertise, there were details missed during the due diligence phase.

What Patrick did not know is that the owner knew his products were soon to be made obsolete. Apple Inc. was going to make changes in the processors they would use and in their operating system. It was these changes, and the lack of motivation to make any investment into modernizing the code, which initiated the owner's willingness to sell the company. Why would he keep it? He didn't want to invest back into it, and he knew that the software was about to become what the industry calls end-of-life.

Most of the code at that time was PowerPC-based, which the Apple Mac line did not understand as a computer language. For almost ten years, the Auto FX software was relying on a computer language emulator that allowed the PowerPC code to translate into readable code on the Mac operating system. The previous owner knew of the issue and knew that by July when Apple would make their changes, this product would be rendered obsolete. It was not until he found this out that he would entertain Patrick's offer to purchase. He even went as far as to make one hard stance on the sale to ensure Patrick would inherit a disaster. The owner told Patrick that he had to have purchased the company by the end of June 2011, or he would not sell. With the venture capital firm leery about these terms, Patrick sought private capital and was able to close the deal within one month. This was all after ten months of pitching for the purchase.

Fourteen days after the buyout was completed, Patrick found himself the owner of a company with no product. Patrick woke up on July 7th, 2011 only to see and hear the unhappy customers file complaints one by one. He discovered he had no working Mac product any longer. The worst part was, there was no guarantee he could ever get it working again. The technology could have been too old and too disjointed to put it back together. Would it even be worth the effort? Would it be possible to pull off? Like all great leaders in times of chaos and adversity, Patrick kept his composure and charted out a direction for his team to attempt a miracle effort.

For the next eighteen months, Patrick had to rally the team to work on a revamp of their product. It needed to be completely re-coded to get the software workable again on the new Mac line. For eighteen months, customers had no access to their product, and many customers threatened to boycott Auto FX products. Patrick and his team stood resolutely and did not give in to the massive weight of adversity and uncertainty. They did not lose faith in Patrick's vision for the company, and the passion of the team carried them through. Even when their customer base thought Auto FX would be shut down, Patrick and his team would persevere.

Then it happened! After sixteen months of herculean effort, Patrick and his team were able to see the interface of their software show up on the screen. It was only one button on a slider, but this was a massive win for the team. It was at this moment they knew they could accomplish a turnaround of the product. For the next two months, the engineers worked rigorously to get all of the other features functional on the new Mac OS. Feature by feature, the product became whole again. After a year and a half, their customers came back, and the revitalized product was well-received.

Turning tragedy into triumph, Patrick and his incredible team have been able to revamp all of their products and grow the business from the 2011 meltdown. Now, after seven years, Patrick and the Auto FX squad are looking to do another revamp of their product. In their first major overhaul, Auto FX was trying to get a workable product which matched the present state of what the hardware and operating systems demanded. In their next revamp, the team is looking to position themselves for significant growth and a notable spot as a leader in the image enhancement and photo editing market. This time, under Patrick's leadership, Auto FX is making those necessary investments and taking advantage of optimized, cutting edge code to outperform their competition.

The whole experience was a harsh lesson in overcoming adversity. The owner took advantage Patrick's friendship and put him in an incredibly difficult position. This selfish act of cowardice and deception is the exact opposite of great leadership. Overcoming adversity is never easy, but great leaders know that achieving anything great will require sacrifice. Not every day is a company purchased, only to see its products become obsolete within a couple of weeks. But even times as desperate as this can be overcome by a great leader who is willing to do what it takes and follow through on the mission they have set out to accomplish.

CHAPTER 6

GREAT LEADERS ALWAYS FOLLOW UP - COMMUNICATION

We've established that great leaders always follow through. What is the difference in following through and following up? The difference is that follow through is an action and follow up is a call to action.

The theme of this chapter is what type of communication deserves repeated follow up and examples of how great leaders exemplify consistent follow up in these main areas.

The first three topics of vision, expectations, and change are the three most critical aspects of what great leaders articulate. However, there are two less visible areas where great leaders go the extra mile in communicating to their people. These two sections include expressing confidence in your people and appreciation for your people.

Communicate Vision

As we discussed in the chapter on how great leaders always follow a vision, they also need their organization to follow that vision. For an organization to operate as intended, it must be organized. The fastest and most efficient way to organize is around a driving purpose, and that goal is summed up in the stated vision for the organization. We now know that the leader needs to have a vision, the organization needs to buy into following that vision, and the question now is how to ensure that actions align with objectives to reach your end goal.

The answer lies in communication. I'm not talking about an email that goes out in January telling your people that you and your executive staff had met six months ago at an offsite retreat and decided that the new vision for the company was such and such. First of all, the vision of the organization is not something that should be changed every year or at all if possible. The strategy may shift, but a good vision should be timeless. I'm not even talking about a yearly reminder at an all-hands meeting led by the executive staff that reinforces the vision and provides the strategy for the year. How many people remember what they ate last Monday for dinner much less what was said at the beginning of the year once they're in the weeds of execution three months later? So, what is the type of communication that is necessary for the vision to stick and for employees to rally around in their day to day decision making? The answer is two-fold.

The role of executive leadership certainly includes communication to the entire organization of what the vision and strategy is. There might even be programs in place to reward employees who have shown exemplary efforts that reflect being "vision-minded." But should we rely on incentive programs, annual in-person communication, or even emails to suffice? Let's be honest. How many of us always read the incredibly long emails from our executives? I'm not saying that executives shouldn't send emails. They should. My argument is that it's just not enough if you want to be as effective as possible.

What is the primary mechanism put in place to strive toward vision fulfillment? The answer is strategy. Who is primarily responsible for driving strategy execution? The individual contributors. Who is responsible for the individual contributors? The front line managers. So where does the vision need to be best understood? Who is intimately leading the front-lines on a daily basis? Who should be consistently articulating and reinforcing the vision, the strategy, and how their team's goals fit into the bigger picture? By now you've probably guessed it. It's the front-line manager.

The take away here is that executive leadership needs to be sure that their vision is understood and internalized throughout the organization, and it is vital for the front lines if the organization is to be successful. Do not assume everyone knows or is bought into your vision. Make sure your people know their purpose.

This is where the communication needs to be most frequent, and this is where the most significant impact will occur. As Scott Sessions once told me, "The principle of *'why'* tells you and others who is important." The vision for an organization is that *why*. If you're not communicating the vision to your people, the unspoken message that you're sending is that your people are not important.

Martin Luther King Jr. displayed a wonderful consistency in how vision should be communicated. In front of large crowds, King presented awe-inspiring speeches that brought the audience to their feet with sounds of clapping and cheering.

However, Martin knew what I shared earlier: it is great to address big crowds with grandiose speeches, but it is another thing to empower the leaders on the front lines with the same vision so that his influence would exponentially increase. In parallel to the famous speeches, there were countless meetings held by King with other leaders of the movement. If proposed tactics or strategies were contrary to the peaceful protest approach of King's campaign, he would quickly point the group back to the vision he had for America's future. That future, in King's mind, would not be realized through violence. The result of the way that Mr. King communicated his vision was that the movement grew, and it grew without always needing the direct influence of King himself. As Craig Groeschel states in his podcast, "Great leaders know that you can either have control or you can have growth, but you cannot have both."[1]

As a leader, you must develop and empower other leaders who are equipped to not only carry out your mission but be able to empower and equip another generation of leaders through the art of effectively communicating your vision. In this way, communication ensures that your vision will continue being pursued through the inspired work of those you leave to succeed you, long after you are gone. This was the legacy that Martin Luther King Jr. left for those who continue to fight for equal rights among all men and women around the world, and this is how any leader must follow to leave behind their own legacy of great leadership.

Communicate Expectations

As a leader of people, it is easy to make assumptions about what you think your people know. One of those things is what you expect of them. It's especially easy for leaders who have been promoted from within their organization and who know the vision, strategy, goals, and objectives so well to assume everyone else around them has the same level of understanding.

I made this mistake a time or two and didn't realize it until I brought up some of my expectations in a meeting with my team. I thought that I would get the occasional eye roll at the repetitiveness of my preaching and the looks of "we know this already," but I didn't. The looks on my team's face told me that I had done a poor job of communicating my expectations up to that point. One of my team members even remarked, "Okay, then I guess I'm on the right track, but it's good to hear it said out loud." I immediately felt the sensation of failure. I had left my team in a state of ambiguity. I assumed that they understood my expectations, but they didn't. They say it is better to be late than never to arrive, but I do wish I had communicated my expectations much clearer, much earlier.

Communicate Change

Hearing the very phrase *"change initiative"* can be like listening to an expletive come out of your child's mouth. It makes you cringe and even ignites a bit of anger. Whereas we should not tolerate filthy language coming out of our children's mouths, we do need to change the perception of change initiatives in the workplace.

Why does change seem so hard to most people? One explanation is that human beings are creatures of habit. But there is a different side of change that is far too understated. People do not dislike change because of change itself. People hate change because they do not see how the value in changing is greater than the ease of staying the same. Help your people understand the importance, how it will affect them, and give them the new direction. If you can do this successfully, then you will have a much higher likelihood of successfully communicating and executing change.

Confidence

As a leader, if you have communicated the vision, your expectations, and changes as they come up, then you are only part of the way to seeing progress made toward your vision. Why is that? Well, your organization must act on what you have communicated.

Going back to the topic of change, people do not resist change, for the most part, due to rebellion. People resist change for one of a few reasons. One of those reasons, which

I have already touched on, is that people often overvalue what they have today and undervalue what they could have tomorrow if they changed.

Secondly, even if your people understand the value in changing, there can be disconnects when it comes to perceived lacked of ability to accomplish what is being asked of them. As a leader, your job is not merely to reiterate the vision, your expectations, and changes. It is also your responsibility to follow up with communications of confidence that your people are capable of doing what it is that you require of them.

People rise to the reputations you give them. People respond to the type of encouragement that is encompassed by confidence. As a leader, you need to let your people know that you hired them for a reason. If they are in the position, then there is a reason for it, and if they were not capable of carrying out what you have asked of them, then you would not be asking it of them in the first place. There is a great story, passed down through the years, of how impactful communicating confidence can be in the life of a person.

One day, young Thomas Edison came home from school with a note. When his mother asked about the letter, he said he didn't read it but was told to give it directly to his mother. Her eyes began to swell with tears as she read the teacher's note. Concerned for what it said, Thomas asked his mother what the teacher had written. She told him it said Thomas was a genius, that the school was not equipped to teach him, and his mother would have to teach him from now on. Edison's mother allowed him to tinker and invent in his time at home, and as we all know, Thomas Edison grew up to be one of the greatest inventors this world has ever known.

Later in life, long after his mother had passed, Thomas found the note his mother had read to him all those years ago. To his surprise, the note did not say what his mother told him it did. What the letter said was Thomas appeared to have a mental disability, the school's staff was not equipped to teach him, and his mother would have to be responsible for educating him from that point on.[2]

The story is a powerful illustration of what communicating confidence does to people. His mother saw passed what others perceived to be a disability to what was a unique trait in her son, not understood by others. Great leaders do that. They find the unique abilities of their people and help bring out those talents to their fullest. How many Thomas Edison's could we unleash on the world if they only heard a few words of confidence from their leader?

Appreciation

There's nothing more damaging to morale and motivation than a lack of appreciation and praise. This is a critical principle of communication when dealing with people. You should praise every improvement, no matter how little it might be. You should appreciate every victory, regardless of how big. Taking time to celebrate and show your appreciation for a job well done will go much further than you can imagine.

On the flipside, leaders should never criticize. This would

be in direct violation of what Scott Sessions calls the "5 C's that every leader must avoid." Criticism is, as we discussed earlier, a sure indicator of an unhealthy culture. Leaders do not criticize to build themselves up or to tear someone else down. Great leaders avoid the path of criticism, choosing instead to coach their people. Coaching is what people need for improvement, and you should always be looking for ways you can coach your people to get better.

I don't understand why a leader would ever criticize a direct report; you hired them! The employer-employee relationship is treated a lot like marriage is today. If things don't work out, we'll just get another one. This is crazy! Like marriage, it takes a significant amount of investment, patience, self-sacrifice, and effort to make things work. There should be a level of due diligence done in the hiring process, but it is the leader's responsibility to provide the love, nurturing, encouragement, and appreciation that their employees need for growth.

In Maslow's hierarchy of needs, the very base level of needs consists of those things that are necessary for life, like food, water, and shelter. I've heard managers tell employees, "be thankful that you have a job." Well, if you only want to appeal to the most base level of a person's needs, then i guess you can say "mission accomplished."

The second level in Maslow's Needs Pyramid is security and safety. Right between the needs of physical safety and security and the first psychological level of belongingness, Maslow should have included a subsection for psychological safety. If your people are being criticized every time they make a mistake, then they will never feel safe to innovate, fail, and try. Even if you're truly a selfish person who doesn't care about the needs of others, think about the impact that this type of environment will have on *you*. The lack of safety in your organization will never allow your people to act autonomously. Guess who will always have someone knocking on their door asking for permission to do something that could be a bit outside of their job description? Do you really want the added stress of making everyone else's decisions for them all day long?

The opposite of criticism and the solution to this dependency culture you've created is love, encouragement, and appreciation. If you've done your job well in the hiring process, in communicating your vision, and expressing your expectations, then a little encouragement, confidence, and appreciation goes a very long way for your employees who are genuinely trying and want to be successful in their role.

CHAPTER 7

GREAT LEADERS ALWAYS FOLLOW UP - CONTINUAL IMPROVEMENT

The mindset of continuous improvement is part of a growth mindset. The opposite of which, a fixed mindset, would have you to believe that you cannot grow, improve, or adapt. By the very definition, a fixed mindset tells you that things are the way they are and they can't be improved. Both of these thoughts are not only false, they are the very thoughts that promote mental, physical, organizational, and societal decay.

In scientific terms, where growth is absent there's death. The only good thing about a fixed mindset is that, like any mindset or attitude, you can change it. You decide, every second of every day, precisely what attitude and what mindset you will choose in any given circumstance.

Great leaders are always looking to improve and to grow. They constantly ask questions like, how can I make this better? They invest time, effort, and money into personal and professional growth. They do the same for their people and their organizations. Again, without growth there is only death. So, there is only one option if you want to be a great leader.

Great Leaders Are Always Learning

In a seminar on growth, John Maxwell challenged me and the others in the audience to learn something new every day. If you're not learning, you're not growing.

When is the last time that you've learned something for the first time? Learning sparks inspiration. New information keeps things fresh. Acquiring knowledge allows you to continually refine and re-define how you do what you do. As a leader, you need to ask yourself, "What did I learn today."

There are more mediums than one can count, offering free or inexpensive avenues of education. For a leader to be great, they must be continually learning, and with the resources available today, there is no excuse preventing us from doing so.

Today, more than ever, employees and leaders alike *must* have the willingness and follow through to continually educate themselves to stay relevant or risk being left behind. In the words of Warren Bennis:

> *Without a desire to learn and the skills to do so, what will happen to the employees of*
>
> *The 21st Century? They will be trampled by the pace of change, according to Adam Downs, writing in Training magazine. Downs suggests*

that the key employee trait will be a willingness to learn. With it, employees will be more likely to adapt as their jobs change as a challenge to be mastered. They will flex and grow, thereby ensuring their own success and the success of the organization.[1]

Knowing how important it is for leaders to continually learn and grow personally and professionally, what are some ways of doing so? It is not a comprehensive list, but I want to share four of the top ways that leaders continue learning and growing.

Education

There are plenty of examples of great leaders who never finished their formal education. Richard Branson, Mark Zuckerberg, and Steve Jobs are a few great examples of such leaders. Although great leadership does not require a degree of any kind, there is still tremendous value in a formal education.

One of the understated benefits of formal education occurs outside the classroom. I remember the first day of my freshman year in college. I finished meeting one of my lab professors in the last class of my day, and as I was driving home, I remember asking myself, "What do I do now?" For the first time, I had no parents expecting me after school. I had no homework to start on. It was the first time I had complete freedom to decide what I would do with my time.

I think I went grocery shopping or something, but it was the beginning of learning how to make decisions on my own.

Great leaders must make decisions, and when young men and women find themselves alone at college, away from their parents or guardians, they are forced into a situation to start making decisions, and lots of them. Outside of these understated benefits, and with the wealth of easily attainable information today, the practicality of everyone going through formal degree programs is diminishing every day.

In a conversation I had with Jason Fedore, Founder of FACEmeeting, we discussed the future of education and his view on the state of education in America. In Jason's words, "The one thing in our world, in our society, and in our economy we hold out in a lock and key scenario is formal education. You have to obtain this degree, go to this school, and pay this amount of money for this access to information or a certain degree. The issue I have with that is if the goal is to create better people, then our system is counterproductive. Because, how do you change people? The way you change people is by giving them access to information."

A formal education is a great start and a great foundation, but not everyone can afford it. Many companies would never hire someone without a degree, and the ironic thing is that the pace of real-world innovation is faster than college curriculums can keep up. Many of the high-demand jobs, today, require knowledge of information which has no degree programs to learn it. There needs to be, and there's starting to be, a disruption in how education is acquired and looked at by organizations. But even beyond that, there are other ways aspiring leaders can educate themselves in a much more efficient and affordable manner. Do not get me wrong; there is value in formal education, both at the undergraduate and graduate levels. But I do strongly contend that the value and the costs are becoming more misaligned every day.

What are the alternatives? Going to or back to school for two to four years is not practical or affordable for most people. Getting your Bachelor's degree is no guarantee of employment, and getting your Master's degree is no guarantee of promotion. Do you take the gamble of putting your family through enormous amounts of student loan debt? Do you roll the dice with little to no guarantees? What are some alternatives?

The Alternatives

Taking a couple of different jobs right out of college, I finally found an organization where I felt I could start my career. Although I had all of the talent necessary to do the job I was given to do, I certainly lacked much of the technical competence and some of the skills required to execute effectively. I knew the learning curve would be steep and being somewhat still fresh out of the learning environment of college, I went back to rigorous study efforts.

The first question I asked myself was, "where am I going to get the information I need and learn the skills necessary to execute this job well?" Like most folks these days, when we have a question, we immediately turn to Google. I started searching for online materials, and in the course of my searches, I found many free online courses. Unlike my formal education, these classes were condensed and to the point. I was able to complete a number of these courses in the first year of my budding career, and my learning curve shortened because of it.

One of the most exciting aspects of my continual learning, outside of that formal environment, was how I was able to immediately apply what I learned. Learn and apply, learn and apply, that was the method for rapid growth and development.

As time has passed, I have a new found love for reading. I challenged myself to read thirty business-related or leadership-related books from the middle of 2016 to the middle of 2017. Three months before my deadline, I had read thirty-five books. Again, I was able to follow that same method of learn and apply. I still follow that method today.

There are endless resources available to us. Leaders of the past would be angry at the wasted resources we do not take advantage of. Great platforms like Coursera offer the desired University education. There are more books in this world than one could read in a lifetime. There are subject matter experts on podcasts who you can listen to and learn from as you drive to and from work. There are in-person and online courses, webinars, and workshops. The list goes on and on, and many of the options are completely free! Like I said before, there is no excuse preventing leaders who want to grow and develop themselves to do so. More than a piece of paper which shows someone is good at listening and test taking, organizations should be looking for leaders who are hungry enough and motivated enough to continually develop themselves, with all of the resources available to them, beyond the information they only partly retained in their University experience.

Experience

You have probably have heard it said that the best way to learn is through experience. In most instances, people are referring to one's personal experience. I believe this is only part of where experience comes from.

In the case of Buba Turner, she was able to attend executive meetings and learn, first hand, how executives articulated their thoughts, the language used by senior management, and how they preferred the delivery of presentations. Because of this indirect experience, through the benefit of observation, Buba was well-equipped when it was her turn to be in those meetings or give those presentations.

Experience can come from many sources, outside of the job in which you find yourself today. If you're in a sales role and want to get experience in marketing, how do you do that? You can volunteer to be part of a marketing project team. You can read a book on marketing. You can take an online course. When that experience is mostly theoretical, you can find ways to put the theory to practice. Create something and market it. When it comes to experience, your limitations are only set by your mindset, imagination, and your willingness to put in the effort.

Mentors

It has been said that the quickest way to learn is from your failures. I strongly disagree with this expression, because it is much better to learn from *other people's* failures rather than waiting to learn from your own. Mentors can share with you their missteps, and through their failures, you can identify the pitfalls or traps that will inevitably pop up along your leadership journey. There have been a couple of occasions where my superiors have pulled me into their office to share with me their recent failures. Hearing about their experience has often left me with insights which I would not have had otherwise.

Mentors do not necessarily have to be people you know, talk to directly, or even be alive today. There are many great leaders and wise men and women who are no longer on this earth but have left behind autobiographies to share their lives and experiences with us. One of those late mentors of mine is Mary Kay. I never had the opportunity to meet her, but I feel like I know her very well through the study of her autobiography. The life she lived and the way she ran her business has made an incredible impact on me and my philosophy of leadership. This is why I have shared examples from her life in this book.

There are many other examples of how you can find "indirect mentors." You can follow thought leaders on a variety of topics through podcasts. One of my favorite podcasts on leadership is Craig Groeschel's Leadership Podcast. Although I have never had the opportunity to meet him, I have been able to learn a lot about leadership from him. I would consider him a mentor, even if he never knows who I am. Having a mentor, whether direct or indirect, offers an excellent opportunity for accelerated growth and learning.

Reinvention

When it comes to continuous improvement, there will be times when you, or your organization, will have to reinvent yourself. In less than two decades from the start of the 21st century, we've seen several industries disrupted. Movie rentals, taxi service, hotels, and several other industries have had companies fall victim to this disruption when they've failed to either adapt or reinvent themselves in response to these disruptive changes. One company that has a long history of continual reinvention is the Finnish company, Nokia.[1]

Nokia is a little over a century and a half old, having been founded in 1865. The company that most people today remember for their incredibly durable cellular phones, started as a single paper mill operation. The founder of Nokia was a Finnish engineer by the name of Fredrik Idestam who named the company after the Nokianvirta River, where his second mill opened. Enjoying almost a full century of growth in the wood pulp industry, Nokia reinvented itself into a company which focused on rubber, cable, forestry, electronics and power generation. The growth that led to becoming a global brand took place over the course of around fifty years after a merger with Finnish Cable Works Ltd.

The next reinvention would come only decades later. In the 1980s, Europe saw opportunities emerge, and new business models become a possibility once the deregulation of the European Telco industry took place. Taking advantage of the resources, talent, and capabilities that Nokia had acquired through Finnish Cable Works, Nokia embarked on their next transformation, Telecommunications. Starting with both the first fully-digital local telephone exchange in Europe and the world's first car phone, Nokia began to position themselves as a leader in Telecommunications. About a decade later, Nokia's vision of leading the Telco ecosystem came to fruition, and Nokia had become a global brand and leader in mobile phones. Although the success was great, Nokia would only enjoy this position for another decade.

As the first decade of the 21st Century was ending, and the emergence of the iPhone was quickly taking over the mobile phone market, Nokia realized that they needed to reinvent itself yet again. Partnering with Siemens in 2007, the Nokia Siemens Network joint venture launched. In 2011, not giving up entirely on the Smartphone market, Nokia partnered with Microsoft to strengthen their diminishing stance in the industry. Only three years later, in 2014, Nokia sold off most of their Devices and Services business to Microsoft and left that space. Their focus now was set on The Internet of Things. This time Nokia would focus on their networks and technologies expertise to help connect people and things.

In 2015, Nokia made another move toward next-generation technologies with their purchase of Alcatel-Lucent. Nokia also acquired Bell Labs, and with all that they had now become, their most recent focus is strengthening their position to potentially be a leader in the Internet of Things industry which is projected to be worth over $400 billion by the year 2020. At NAB 2017, I even had the chance to meet with some of the Nokia team working in their Ozo division. Nokia Ozo focuses on another trending technology of the 21st Century, virtual reality. It's clear, based on the acquisitions, sell-offs, partnerships, and actions taken by Nokia, that their position is to focus on emerging technologies and leverage their rich history of reinvention to get out ahead of the curve to once again lead another industry.

Would Nokia even be a known entity today if they had remained a wood pulp company like back in the 1800s? My guess is they probably would not. There are not many companies who have a story of reinvention quite like Nokia, and an interesting trend to point out is the time lapse between reinventions for Nokia.

The first reinvention came after a century. The second happened after half a century. The next after only decades. Next it was only one decade. Now, reinventing itself is taking less than three years between shifts.

The trend with Nokia is consistent with the blazing speed at which many industries are now shifting, and companies are quickly having to reinvent themselves to keep up. The Cloud, the IoT, the Network, and a host of other factors are driving many of these changes, but even industries that are traditionally not high tech are being disrupted by the pace of innovation through vehicles like the internet and smart devices. Not only physical products and business models but supply chain innovation is driving companies to think differently about how they do business. The point is that businesses today do not have the luxury that Nokia did in the 1800s with having over a century to reinvent itself after their first success. In the 21st Century, the only constant is constant change.

Fruit of Failure

In the absence of failure, growth is absent or minimal. People often say that you learn more from your failures than you do from your successes. I believe that sentiment is correct, with one caveat. Failure without reflection, followed by course correction, is doomed to repeat itself.

Think about the start of every year. Gym memberships spike for a couple of months, and then the crowds of people slowly dwindle. Why do people make such half-hearted attempts at their New Year's resolution? Well, anytime someone takes on a challenge that is new, demanding, and taxing, there is pain involved. Most people do not enjoy pain. And what it boils down to is your mindset. In business, great leaders expect painful moments. Organizations will go through "growing pains," just as your body goes through growing pains from physical exercise. And just like physical exercise, your business, like your body, will not see significant results if you are not pushing yourself to the point of failure. If you never fail at anything, then you are most likely not pushing your limits or testing your capacity for growth. Nothing significant gets accomplished by going through the motions of what is comfortable or easy.

Great leaders not only know that failure is never final, but they also know that failure is necessary. Again, the fruit of failure comes from your mindset. If you want failure to bear good fruit, then you must see any failure as an opportunity to learn and improve. As we discussed before, great leaders are biased toward action. They do not wait around to make perfect decisions. Great leaders make decisions, learn, and adjust along the way. Expecting failures will allow leaders to stay focused on the end goal.

Learning from failure is one of the critical traits of a great leader. Many great leaders whom I have had the opportunity to speak with or interview are strong proponents of having a process. In their view, great leaders must have a process to sustain a great organization. If you look at football coaches like Bill Belichick and Nick Saban, they too are big on process and executing on that process. Whether in business or sports, every process goes through refinement. Even great leaders who are running successful organizations know that constant reevaluation and improvement is necessary? Why? As time goes on, things change. As things evolve, there might be parts of the process that become outdated. Since great leaders follow indicators, great leaders will look at indicators of failing processes to adjust as early as possible.

Once you start focusing on the failure as anything other than an opportunity to learn and grow, you will begin to bear bad fruit. Failure does not define you, and people are not failures. Failures are simply one-time events. The only way that a failure causes real damage is if there are moral, ethical, or legal failures which cripple organizations, careers, and reputations. Outside of those times, failure will not define you unless you stop viewing failure as a one-time event and start viewing it as a state of being. It all comes down to mindset.

CHAPTER 8

HOW GREAT LEADERS ALWAYS FOLLOW

This world is in grave need of a new type of leadership. We can point to all of the infamous cases like Enron, WorldCom, and a host of others that have led us to a dilemma where organizational leaders are now often viewed with skepticism. Business leaders have to work harder than ever to not only run successful businesses through rapid innovation and disruption, but they are also striving to prove that they are running them ethically. You can follow all seven of the principles we've already outlined, but if you do not know *how* to follow, then you risk losing everything.

Values Are Not Situational

The values of an organization need to be established by the leader of the organization, and they need to be unwavering. Values cannot be situational, and they must be enforced to be meaningful. I love the saying, "If you don't stand up for something, you will fall for anything." Everyone needs a "North Star" that guides the decisions and direction that we take. Without direction, we will get nowhere.

I grew up in a small town in Louisiana and attended a private, Christian high school. Each year, one of my required credits was a Bible class. Being a follower of Jesus and growing up in church, I liked having that opportunity. However, one of my classes was Situational Ethics. I hated that class. Growing up, I was always quiet and reserved, but I could not keep quiet in this class. It might be that the teacher ran it poorly, but the question of right and wrong being determined by your situation irritated me. My grades were lower than they should have been, and I was the farthest from the "teacher's pet." I've always been a deep thinker, but in this class, my thoughts came flowing out as I vigorously debated with my teacher. I admit that my passion for the topics we discussed might have come across as disrespectful towards my teacher, but I still firmly cling to the fact that right and wrong, or ethics, is *not* determined by your situation.

Scott Sessions and the other members of the executive leadership team at Mountain Alarm exemplify the definition of integrity and run their organization by a set of deeply ingrained values. They live with a set of deep convictions, morals, and values that are not swayed by the false concept of "situational ethics." Scott told me a great story of a time when their President and CEO, Rodney Garner, had an opportunity to skirt the lines of ethics but held firm to their values.

Early on in the history of the company, Mountain Alarm had executed work worth about $20,000 for a large construction company in Utah. After the work was completed,

Payroll came in to talk to Rodney about $15,000 they needed in order to pay a pending bill. Rodney was curious as to why she was bringing this to his attention directly. She went on to let him know that they were paid double by Big-D, the construction company, and they needed that extra $20,000 to pay their $15,000 bill. She started to suggest that they could hold the money until they could recoup the $15,000 and pay Big-D back later, but Rodney didn't entertain the notion for a moment. Very swiftly he said, "Send it back, right now."

Now that sets a cultural tone. When the CEO acts with that level of integrity and moral astuteness, what message do you think that sends to the rest of the organization? Did Rodney decide that the situation of being behind financially made it okay to hold onto money that wasn't theirs and pay it back later? Do you think Big-D would have even known? Rodney didn't care. His deep-rooted value system told him that regardless the situation, taking something not earned was stealing, and there was no situation which would condone stealing.

When Scott told me that they hire and fire based on the principles of Intelligence, Initiative, and most importantly Integrity, the tone set by their CEO stands as the beacon of accountability to enforce that type of culture. This is why it is so important for organizations to have deeply ingrained values for their organization and hire and fire based on those values. Skills can be taught, but values are almost impossible to change.

Character

One of the best definitions of character I have grown up with is, "doing what is right, even when it is not the popular thing to do." There will be times, if you have not experienced them yet, when you will face leadership decisions which will challenge your character. In a world where right is called wrong and wrong is called right, it can be easy to give into the trends of this age and act against your character. Great leaders know this is unacceptable. Some of the most celebrated leaders in the history of humankind are and were men and women of incredibly high morals and character.

Rex Rollo, who we've talked about a couple of times already, is one of those leaders who sticks to his morals and whose actions are consistent with his morals and ethics. In the housing market crash during the great recession of 2008, a large part of the problem was that loans were being issued based on someone's promise of what income they had and what they said they could afford. There were no checks and balances, and most financial institutions did not care. The temptation to make money outweighed sound, moral decision making on what was right for the person and the company. Rex liked to refer to these loans as "liar loans."

There were branches of America First coming to Rex asking him why they could not make the same loans that local competitors were making. His answer was, "I don't know how *they* are making those loans to begin with." It went against everything Rex knew to be true, and he refused to give those type of loans to people.

There were times when the regulators went into the

America First offices and told the board their company was headed in the wrong direction. He looked at the regulators, and he looked at the board and said, "I'll take full responsibility for the regulator." In Rex's belief system, great leaders make decisions, and they take responsibility for those decisions. They own them. Great leaders have resolute character, and they live by the adage by Alexander Hamilton, "those who stand for nothing will fall for anything."

Have a Heart

There is a common expression used when it comes to influence: "People do not care how much you know until they know how much you care." Since leadership is about influence, people must know that you care about them. One of the qualities of great leaders is empathy. Great leaders have a heart for people and genuinely care about the lives of those they serve. Jason Fedore shared with me an incredible story of how one great leader changed the life of a man and his family by choosing to have a heart.

When Jason was a chiropractor, before founding FACEmeeting, he had a patient who he could tell had a good work ethic. Jason had many conversations with this gentleman, and he enjoyed the time he was able to spend with the man.

As Jason got to know him, he found out that the man was living in a small apartment with his wife and two kids. They were broke. The apartment was very cheap, not nice, and very small. The gentleman had been getting by in caring for his family by doing whatever handyman repair work he could find. Knowing his situation, Jason hardly charged the man anything for the work he had done.

This gentleman, looking for a change, got the idea that he wants to own a franchise of a company called Insulright. Insulright is a spray-in home insulation company which operates through a franchising model. One day, the man got into his car, and he drove to Ohio to meet the founder.

When he got to Ohio and found the company, he was acting in pure faith. He was able to meet with the founder, and he began by telling the founder, "I am here. I have no money and nothing to invest in this, but I want to do this." The founder, a multi-million dollar success, with several successfully operating franchises, sat him down and began to ask him questions. He asked the gentleman, "Where do you want to go? What are you trying to accomplish?"

After the man explained what he wanted to do, the founder said, "you know what, I'm going to help you. I'll help you get a truck; I'll help you get started. I'll get all of the materials you need to get started, and you can pay me after your first job. And if you do well and keep things straight, I am going to help you expand and grow your business." And that was the start of a new career for this man.

After only one year, Jason noticed the man showing up to his appointments dressed a little nicer, and he started paying a little more for his adjustments. One day, when he came in for his adjustment, Jason asked him, "Hey man, what's going on? It seems like things are going well for you, and it's great to see you happy." It was then where the gentleman began to tell Jason his story and the significant change he made in his life. Now this man was able to afford the franchise license, he was able to buy a new truck, and this once broke handyman is a multi-millionaire still living in Pittsburg with around sixty employees. Talk about a turnaround!

With such an incredible success story, it is easy to forget that this man did not get to become a millionaire all on his own. He had help, and the particular help he needed was the help he received. If it wasn't for the heart of the founder, this man might still be living in a small apartment with his wife and two kids and still just trying to survive. It takes a leader with a heart to give someone help, to see beyond the surface and invest in someone's potential. The founder could have given him the materials he needed and said "good luck," but he didn't. It would have still been a thoughtful and generous gesture, but he went beyond that. He also invested his time, energy, and experience into this man and put him on a path to succeed and grow. That is the real heart of leadership.

Humility

With any success comes the opportunity to give into pride. As we wrap things up, this is a great section to tell you a little of my story, but it is not because I consider myself to be the ultimate example of humility. The reason I want to share part of my life with you is to share how I try to avoid those moments when pride tries to cloud my thoughts and dictate my actions. The method, which I will unveil later, is the important part.

I grew up in a rural town in southern Louisiana. I lived

on a one-acre plot of land, surrounded by three soybean fields and a sugarcane field. My father worked and still works, for the Federal Government, and my mother is a bank teller. Our family did not have a lot of disposable income, and the extra we did have went to pay for my siblings and me to have a private school education. For anyone not familiar with public schools in Louisiana, most are not close to what I received at my private school.

My father taught me an important leadership trait from an early age. I saw the sacrifices he made for our family, and I saw a man who spent his life working hard at home and in his profession to provide and care for his family. My father wanted a Toyota Tundra for at least fifteen years. When he did make a new car purchase, it was usually to give my mother something better to drive since she took my siblings and me everywhere. One time he did purchase his Tundra, but he felt bad and brought it back so that my mom could have the new car in the family. Trust me, this sacrifice and putting his family before him did not go unnoticed.

I played many sports growing up, but my two favorites were basketball and baseball. My first love was basketball, but I was honestly a better baseball player. When college basketball did not work out for me, some of my fraternity brothers at McNeese State convinced me to join the cheer squad. Little did I know at the time that this decision would change the course of my life.

Going into my senior year of college, I did not like the way I was living, and I wanted to quit cheer to focus on my future. Taking the advice of my father, I decided to finish out my last year on the squad. I'm thankful that I did. The one thing I was looking forward to about cheer that year was that we were going to play Texas A&M. We played LSU my sophomore year, and I couldn't wait to be in another Southeastern Conference stadium.

Well, since it would be the first year Texas A&M joined the SEC, they had to revise their schedule. This meant that McNeese would no longer be part of their schedule, and we would have to find somewhere else to play or have an extra bye-week.

Of all places, McNeese found out that Weber State, in Ogden Utah, had an opening for the same week we were supposed to play Texas A&M. I had no clue what was in Utah, nor did I know what was in store for me there.

We flew into the small Ogden Airport, and we took the bus down 24th Street to our hotel. I remember crossing the 24th Street Bridge and thinking, "Man, this looks like a place where movies are shot." Much to my surprise, I found out later that several movies have been filmed in downtown Ogden.

The next day, as the game was in full swing, I saw a beautiful woman walk across the bleachers in front of me. To keep the story short, her mom and my cheer coach met during the game. At halftime, my coach thought I should meet her, and she introduced me. After talking the entire twenty-minute halftime, I got her number, and three months later I found myself flying back to Ogden to propose.

We got married a month after I graduated college, and life has been great ever since. Well, that's how the story should go, right? In reality, I moved 2,000 miles away with only $500 to my name (Hey, I was a recent college grad, I thought it was awesome that I had zero student loan debt). I had my degree, why wouldn't I get a job right away, in a new town, with zero connections?

It would be months before I would get my first job, and I waited tables to make ends meet for my new family. I not only had a wife to provide for, but I also had an eight-year-old daughter who I was blessed to inherit when I married my wife. It was a scary time in my life. I was supposed to be the provider, and I was struggling to do one of the things I felt was most important for me to be doing.

After eight months of waiting tables and six months of teaching high school, I knew I was not following my passions, and teaching was not going to be my career. In Louisiana, my job was going to be in Insurance. My grandfather had his own insurance business, and I was in line to take over for him. He wasn't too happy when I moved away, but I think he eventually forgave me.

It was this moment in my life when I found myself continually praying for something that would give my family all that it needed to thrive and that meshed my passions and talents. I remembered the sacrifices my father made, and I was willing to do what it took to make sure my family was provided for, but I wanted to give them all of the things I had growing up and more.

It was this time when a friend told me about MarketStar Corporation. Their headquarters was only six miles from my house. I thought it sounded like a cool place, and my friend would go on and on about how great the culture was, how family oriented the company was, and how there were many great career opportunities there. I was intrigued. I also needed insurance coverage with the Affordable Care Act looming and the threat of penalties if I didn't have coverage. My teaching job didn't provide coverage, and they didn't pay me enough to buy my own.

I look back at a rough start to my life as an adult, but my family and I are now in a really good spot. My career got off to a great start, and I've been blessed to find a role where I have been able to excel and grow with the organization. There are times when I feel underpaid or like I am capable of holding positions that are above me, and these are those pride-filled moments I was referring to earlier. The successes I've found have, at times, led me to think more highly of myself than I should. It is these times when I reflect back on my past.

Looking back, I remember that I am a simple country kid from Louisiana who grew up surrounded by bean fields. I remember that I moved to a new state with only $500 in my pocket. I don't have an Ivy League education, and I do not come from an area where high-tech jobs the first thought when it comes to career choices. But to now be representing a large, high-tech company, to experience tremendous professional and career growth within the organization, and doing things I would have never dreamed of, I can only look back and be grateful for where I am today.

That is the secret of humility: remaining grateful. Even if you aspire to be the CEO of a company or launch a highly successful startup, even if you achieve all you have set out to do, remaining in a state of gratefulness is what keeps you grounded. None of us chose who our parents were, where we were born, what color skin we have, or what our natural talents would be, but we all can be great. Whether you were born into privilege or rose from poverty, knowing that you had no choice in the matter should keep you grateful for where you are today. Great leaders are humble, and it is impossible to be arrogant when you remain in a state of gratefulness. In the words of my favorite Lecrae song, "if you want to be great, drop the 'e' to the end and add 'ful' to it."

Serve To Lead

Servant leadership is the focus of great leaders. Just as Jesus came to serve, great leaders have the mentality of a servant leader, regardless of their title. In the words of Rex Rollo, "You can say you are a great leader, but it is the team you have working for you." Rex understands what all great leaders understand about leadership. It is all about influence. We've already established that a command and control culture is not one employed by great leaders. Why is that? Great leaders know that people hate being told what to do "because I am the boss, and I say so." But what happens when every member of your team knows you have their best interest in mind?

When leaders understand their role, they know that leadership is much more about serving the people and the greater good of the organization than it is about wielding power or giving orders. Great leaders go to lengths to give their future leaders the opportunity to grow and develop. They go to bat for their people, and they never talk with condescension about or toward their people.

By nature, leadership is all about serving. Your role becomes more focused on developing others the higher up the ladder you go. In your leadership progression, you will go through several stages of leadership development, not only for yourself but for others. First, you will develop others to do their jobs well. Then, you will develop others into leaders who can teach others to do their jobs well. Next, you will develop leaders who can develop other leaders. As you go further up, it becomes much less about you and much more about the exponential growth you can drive for your organization through the development of all those people you have within your scope of influence.

If you look at any great leader, whether it be Mary Kay, Martin Luther King Jr., or Jesus, they were completely focused on serving the needs of others. Not one of the world's greatest leaders ever set out looking for fame. They set out looking to make a difference, to add value to others, and to change the world. As you reflect upon the key ideas in this book, I want you to walk away asking yourself the questions every leader should ask. How can you leverage your talents to make a difference? Who can you serve? How can you add value to the lives of others? Who and what will you start to follow? How can you change the world?

NOTES

Introduction:

1   BibleGateway. (n.d.). Retrieved October 12, 2017, from https://www.biblegateway.com/passage/?search=Exodus%2B20%3A11&version=KJV
2   "BibleGateway." Matthew 15:14 KJV - - Bible Gateway,www.biblegateway.com/passage/?search=Matthew%2B15%3A14&version=KJV.
3   Palmer, A. (2017, August 08). Intel CEO Brian Krzanich Reveals Some of His Best Leadership Tips. Retrieved October 12, 2017, from
4   https://www.thestreet.com/story/14258099/1/intel-ceo-brian-krzanich-s-top- leadership-tips.html

Chapter 1:

1   Bort, J. (2013, September 11). Mark Zuckerberg: 'Bill Gates Was My Hero'. Retrieved October 13, 2017, from http://www.businessinsider.com/mark-zuckerberg-bill- gates-was-my-hero-2013-9
2   Facebook. (n.d.). Retrieved October 13, 2017, from https://www.facebook.com/pg/facebook/about/
3   BibleGateway. (n.d.). Retrieved October 15, 2017, from https://www.biblegateway.com/passage/?search=Proverbs%2027:17
4   Blanchard, K., & Hodges, P. (2007). Lead Like Jesus. Thomas Nelson Inc.
5   Groeschel, C. (201). Craig Groeschel Leadership Podcast [Video blog post]. Retrieved from https://www.life.church/leadershippodcast/

Chapter 2:

1   Jim Donald (businessman). (2017, September 01). Retrieved October 13, 2017, from https://en.wikipedia.org/wiki/Jim_Donald_(businessman)

Chapter 3:

1   Jobs, S. (2005, June). Speech presented at Stanford Commencement Speech in Stanford University, Stanford, Ca.
2   Porter, M. (n.d.). TOP 25 QUOTES BY MICHAEL PORTER. Retrieved October 13, 2017, from http://www.azquotes.com/author/11790-Michael_Porter
3   Flamm, M. C. (n.d.). George Santayana (1863—1952). Retrieved October 13, 2017, from http://www.iep.utm.edu/santayan/
4   Grove, A. S. (1999). Only The Paranoid Survive. Doubleday.
5   Bowman, N., Bonchek, M., Vermeulen, F., & Wittenburg, M. R. (2017, May 03). 4 Ways to Improve Your Strategic Thinking Skills. Retrieved October 13, 2017, from https://hbr.org/2016/12/4-ways-to-improve-your-strategic-thinking-skills
6   Groeschel, C. (2016, August 31). Craig Groeschel Leadership Podcast - Leading Up [Video blog post]. Retrieved from https://www.life.church/leadershippodcast/leading- up-part-1/
7   Groeschel, C. (2016, August 31). Craig Groeschel Leadership Podcast - Leading Up [Video blog post]. Retrieved from https://www.life.church/leadershippodcast/leading- up-part-1/
8   Kennedy, J. F. (1961, January 20). John F. Kennedy's Inaugural Address. Speech presented at Presidential Inaugural Address, Washington D.C.

Chapter 5:

1   Google Dictionary. (n.d.). Retrieved October 14, 2017, from https://www.google.com/search?q=definition%2Bof%2Bdiscipline&rlz=1C1GGRV_enUS751US755&oq=definition%2Bof%2Bdiscipline&aqs=chrome.0.0l6.4177j0j7&sourceid=chrome&ie=UTF-8
2   Responsibly Grown and Fair Trade Coffee. (n.d.). Retrieved October 14, 2017, from https://www.starbucks.com/responsibility/sourcing/coffee

Chapter 6:

1. Groeschel, C. (2016). Craig Groeschel Leadership Podcast - Leading Up [Video blog post]. Retrieved from https://www.life.church/leadershippodcast/
2. Team, E., & Elmore, T. (2017, July 31). EntreLeadership - #215: Dr. Tim Elmore—Meet Generation Z [Audio blog post]. Retrieved from https://www.entreleadership.com/podcasts/215-dr-tim-elmoremeet- generation-z

Chapter 7:

1. Our history. (n.d.). Retrieved October 14, 2017, from https://www.nokia.com/en_int/about-us/who-we-are/our-history

www.ingramcontent.com/pod-product-compliance
Lightning Source LLC
Chambersburg PA
CBHW020441220526
45464CB00002B/806